ARBITRARY DEATH

A PROSECUTOR'S PERSPECTIVE ON THE DEATH PENALTY

D1311047

RICK UNKLESBAY

Arbitrary Death: A Prosecutor's Perspective on the Death Penalty

Published by Wheatmark®
2030 East Speedway Boulevard, Suite 106
Tucson, Arizona 85719 USA
www.wheatmark.com

ISBN: 978-1-62787-680-3 (paperback)
ISBN: 978-1-62787-681-0 (ebook)
LCCN: 2019932999

Bulk ordering discounts are available through Wheatmark, Inc. For more information, email orders@wheatmark.com or call 1-888-934-0888.

TO SURVIVORS

———

*All author proceeds from the sale of this book
go directly to benefit Homicide Survivors Inc. of Tucson.
Azhomicidesurvivors.org is a nonprofit organization that provides
emotional support, financial assistance, and courtroom advocacy
to the families and loved ones of homicide victims at no cost.
Established in 1982, Homicide Survivors has provided support for
hundreds of survivors of homicide victims and has
advocated for laws advancing victims' rights.*

CONTENTS

FOREWORD

In 1971, I became the first law clerk for newly appointed Justice Lewis F. Powell Jr. In the first six months of his service on the United States Supreme Court, Justice Powell was required to confront directly the question whether the death penalty, as administered in this country at that time, was constitutional. In June 1972, after devoting a tremendous amount of time and effort, Justice Powell concluded with confidence that the death penalty was indeed an acceptable form of punishment. In so concluding, he became one of the justices then in the minority. As has now been reported in a number of scholarly accounts, Justice Powell was deeply disappointed. Four years later, however, Justice Powell again had the opportunity to focus on the death penalty, and this time his view prevailed. By 1976, Justice Powell's views became firmly rooted and reflected the views of a majority of the Court.

From those days, over the remainder of his career as a Supreme Court justice—another eleven years—Justice Powell consistently supported the death penalty under virtually every circumstance. Years later, however, his biographer, while interviewing the retired justice, discovered that he had come to conclude that the death penalty was wrong constitutionally and as a matter of public policy. When I learned of the justice's change of mind, I said to myself that there could hardly be in my lifetime a more stunning reversal of opinion.

I have now discovered another and possibly even more profound change of opinion with respect to the death penalty. The book you are about to read tells an account of a professional career every bit as deeply connected to capital punishment as was Justice Powell's. Rick Unklesbay has been a prosecuting attorney in

Arizona for almost forty years. He has personally prosecuted well over one hundred homicide cases, and in at least twenty of those, he and his office sought the death penalty. In these chapters he traces nine of those cases. The cases themselves are notable, but they also all arose from what most readers will agree are horrific circumstances—facts that most readers will see as heinous and deserving the ultimate punishment. They also have in common—as with many death penalty cases—the realities of a lengthy trial and extensive post-conviction history. Throughout all these cases—many of them spanning more than twenty years—Rick Unklesbay pursued the death penalty. At no point in any of these cases, or other cases handled by him and members of his office, was there even the slightest indication that his views on the propriety of the death penalty might have waivered.

Now, Rick Unklesbay is sharing with the readers of this book his reasons for no longer believing that the death penalty should be sustained. In my mind, his transformation may well exceed Justice Powell's. Justice Powell has been criticized many times for waiting until after he retired to disclose his changed opinion. I have no doubt that Rick Unklesbay will be met with criticism—criticism that is sure to come from, among others, prosecutors and defense lawyers. For all who may react critically, I urge you to give this book a careful read. The topic and the author deserve that much.

Rick Unklesbay has a well-earned reputation as a prosecutor and leader in Arizona's legal professional community. He rose to the top of the Pima County Attorney's Office and has remained above reproach throughout some tumultuous years in which the performance of other death penalty prosecutors in that office have come under serious criticism. He has also served as an adjunct member of the University of Arizona College of Law faculty and has often been sought out to speak at seminars and legal education programs.

I am one of the criminal defense lawyers who has litigated

against Rick Unklesbay, and indeed one of the cases in this book is one in which I was counsel on the other side. Based upon my own intense personal experience in that case, as confirmed by countless professional encounters in other circumstances, I have long regarded Rick Unklesbay as the best and most highly ethical prosecutor I have encountered.

Rick Unklesbay now chairs his office's Conviction Integrity Unit—the first and still only prosecutorial office in Arizona that has adopted a program to assist in the review of cases of possible injustice. He joins Justice Powell among the finest and most conscientious legal minds I have encountered. Unlike Justice Powell, however, Rick Unklesbay does not purport in these pages to offer his view on the constitutionality of the death penalty. As you read his conclusions, you may come to decide for yourself whether the death penalty, as he has seen and lived it, has become a form of unconstitutionally cruel and unusual punishment.

Whether constitutionally viable or not, consideration of the cases discussed in these chapters lays bare the challenges of capital prosecution. It is also worth pondering this reality. When Rick Unklesbay began doing death penalty trials in Arizona, his office had a well-deserved reputation as the most aggressive jurisdiction seeking the death penalty in this state. Today, however, there are virtually no death penalty cases pending in Pima County.

My biases are evident. I am not comfortable with the death penalty in any case. No matter what one's views, however, this book deserves close attention. My hope is that it will become part of the standard curriculum for undergraduate and law school students studying this country's criminal laws. It is an honor to be associated with this text.

Larry A. Hammond
Phoenix, Arizona

ACKNOWLEDGMENTS

Larry Hammond is an attorney in Phoenix with the firm of Osborn Maledon. Although he has a busy practice, he made time to found the Arizona Justice Project and also helped found the Arizona Capital Representation Project. I'm proud to call him friend. For a year before publication, Larry gave me incredible support and many recommendations on the completion of this manuscript. I am forever indebted to him.

Stephen Bright has a national reputation for defending people facing the death penalty. He teaches at Yale Law School and directed the Southern Center for Human Rights for thirty-five years. Steve was so very generous with his time in giving recommendations about the content of the manuscript. I am very grateful.

Professor James W. Clarke of the University of Arizona was one of the first people I consulted with about the book. Professor Clarke is the author of several books on both true crime as well as fictional crime. His advice was both helpful and inspiring.

Along the way so many people gave feedback, recommendations, and advice for which I am also grateful. Professor Robert Glennon of the James Rogers School of Law at the University of Arizona and the Honorable Karen Adam (ret.) took time away from teaching law in China to give me advice. Author, journalist, and professor Tom Zoellner generously gave me much needed advice and encouragement despite having never met me. My friend Mark Kimble offered support and advice. The Honorable Pete Eckerstrom of the Arizona Court of Appeals provided me context and clarity for my writing. Laura Udall, a criminal defense attorney, has provided insight about the manuscript for over a year. My wife, Margaret Norem, gave not only support and encouragement, but she also lent her editing skills to the early drafts. Finally, the survivors of the victims in these chapters allowed use of the photographs of their loved ones and gave me inspiration for writing this book. The brave and remarkable manner in which they carried on with life after a devastating loss was not just inspiring during the litigations and trials of these cases, but it continues to be so when I periodically see them in the community. I thank each of them for their support.

PROLOGUE

On November 8, 2000, I stood and watched while a man died. I did not intervene in any way. In fact, I was the person most responsible for his death. At three o'clock that day, I stood with several others in a crowded and cramped observation room and silently watched while Don J. Miller was put to death by the State of Arizona in the prison execution chamber in Florence by lethal injection. Afterward, I got into my car and drove the hour back to Tucson where I live and have prosecuted cases for over three decades.

Normally I have sympathy for others and the suffering in their lives that caused them to be the person they are, but I had no pity for Miller as he lay strapped to his gurney. Eight years before, Miller had taken a gun and put five bullets in the head of a nineteen-year-old woman who had already been shot once by Joe Luna, the father of her infant child. The victim wanted fifty dollars a month for diapers and baby food, and Luna and Miller decided murder was an easier way to handle the matter. They killed in cold blood, taking the life of an innocent teenager and leaving her infant motherless and, with the conviction of Luna, parentless.

It was not the first, or the last, execution that I attended as a prosecutor, being one of the official witnesses that Arizona law requires be present at state-sanctioned killings. But it was the execution that began my journey of asking why we still employ the death penalty. Since Miller's execution, I've prosecuted many more murder cases in which the state sought the death penalty and have been witness to other executions. Each case I tried took me back to Miller's death, and with the conclusion of those subsequent trials where the death penalty was imposed, it caused me to question even more the reasons we continue to seek the ultimate punishment.

The perspective I have is, I think, different than most who write about the death penalty. I am neither an abolitionist nor an ardent supporter of capital punishment. My perspective is unique in that I'm someone who has prosecuted numerous death penalty cases, who has several defendants currently on death row in Arizona, and who has had two defendants I prosecuted be put to death. It is an experience that rejects the notion asserted by some opponents of capital punishment that prosecutors often get it wrong but is also an experience that causes me to recognize that the death penalty system can be arbitrary no matter how hard prosecutors try to make it work. The randomness inherent in capital punishment should lead us to rid it from our statutes, as no matter what systemic changes we might make, the decisions leading to a death sentence are not much different from a roll of the dice.

My intent with this writing is to demonstrate to whom the death penalty applies and, perhaps just as important, to whom it does not. I doubt that opponents of the death penalty will find any surprises here and will feel as though I've only scratched the surface of the problems associated with capital punishment. Some ardent supporters will no doubt feel I have betrayed them by writing that we should rid ourselves of a punishment we simply don't need. Still others will think me a hypocrite for expressing these views while still prosecuting these cases. They are probably all correct.

———

This book is really for those who haven't given much thought to the death penalty but are generally in favor of keeping it as part of our criminal justice system. Much is never covered about the decision-making process of the prosecutor, the taxpayer-funded defense, the lengthy delays in just getting to trial, and the even longer delays in carrying out the sentence.

To illustrate the evolution of my thinking on the death penalty, I've chosen a number of cases I've prosecuted over the years that demonstrate how our capital system works, or doesn't, and how the death penalty applied to these cases. One's opinion on capital punishment tends to be very personal but is often shaped only by tales of horrible murders on the one side or by stories of exonerations of the innocent on the other. Few people outside prosecutors, defense attorneys, and the judges who work these cases have much idea of what really happens. I hope to shed some light on that process and allow readers to make better-informed decisions.

My opinions are just that, my own thoughts on capital punishment. I don't speak for my office on this matter, although there are other prosecutors here that share my views and some who are avid opponents of the death penalty. A friend who has been a judge for many years, Teresa Godoy, recently told me that, if published, my opinions might be used by the defense in pending cases. While I don't think my opinions have much relevance to any legal matter before the court, I do hope they stir some debate about our continued use of this punishment.

The titles of the chapters dealing with a specific case are named for the victim, the person who had no voice in the prosecution of their murder. I mean to honor their memory by using their names and hope the surviving families see it that way also. I knew none of the victims of course, having entered the cases upon their deaths, or in some cases decades later. But in each case I felt I got to know the victim through their family. Each family had a lifelong impact on me. From the parents and brother of a young student named Susan who asked me not to seek the death penalty in her name, as she was the college campus president of Amnesty International, to the mother of a cab driver named Timothy who was so relieved to see a life sentence instead of the death penalty imposed, to the parents of seven-year-old Rhia, who were kind and gracious throughout the years it took to bring Rhia's killer to justice, each family affected me in ways I could never forget.

Each story is very different than the next. But each case, and the surviving family members they affected, had the common experience of being subjected not just to the frailties of the criminal justice system, but to the vagaries of the complex and arbitrary system we call capital punishment.

When I started law school in 1977 at the University of Arizona, I had no idea what the practice of law was all about. I had been substitute teaching the year prior and soon realized I was not cut out to be a teacher. So I applied to law school, never having met a lawyer in my life. It was a struggle. After doing poorly in my first semester, one professor suggested I look for another field of study, as he felt I wasn't cut out to be a lawyer. While I was not doing well, I stuck out the year and then decided to keep going, although I had no idea where I was headed.

Over the three years of law school, I felt lost most of the time. Contracts, torts, and labor law were completely foreign to me. Not that I was alone in that, but I seemed to flounder and felt perhaps the first-semester law professor may have been right. While I figured out how to survive school, the prospect of spending my career actually practicing any of these areas of law was making me regret going at all.

It wasn't until my third year of school that I discovered the courtroom. The state supreme court allowed third-year law students, under the supervision of actual lawyers, to try cases in court. I signed up for the prosecution clinic in city court where misdemeanor cases were taken to trial. A semester of that and I was hooked. Trial work was exciting and terrifying and was the only thing in law school that finally made sense to me. Standing in front of a jury and arguing facts was more comprehensible than discussing case law in a classroom. Somewhat naively I decided I'd become a trial lawyer.

After graduation and passing the bar (a feat that still amazes me to this day, given my performance in law school) I started looking for a job in criminal law, the only place you could be assured you were going to get in front of a jury. At the time I didn't really care which side of the aisle I'd end up on. I interviewed with the public defender, private lawyers in a criminal practice, and prosecutor's offices around the state.

Typically, in law school students spend summers as a law clerk in a private law office or public agency to get real-world experience. I never did that. Instead, I spent my summers working as a laborer at an open pit copper mine in order to make enough money to go back to school in the fall. It paid more than clerking, and it was the only way I could afford to stay in school. As a result I didn't have the legal experience other students had or the connections to law offices in which they'd gained experience. So I had some tough competition in seeking work. I spent several months after graduation working as a clerk and doing legal research for a couple of local criminal defense attorneys in Tucson. Finally, a year after graduation, the Pima County Attorney offered me a job as a prosecutor. I started on July 1, 1981.

I thought I'd get three to four years of trial experience, work at it until the novelty of trial work wore off, and then get a job in private practice. I never did. The adrenaline rush of being in the courtroom simply never waned. As I gained experience, my cases became more serious, and within two or three years, I was prosecuting homicide cases. I'd found what I wanted to do.

———

Even beyond the excitement of trying a case, I felt like I was making a difference in people's lives. I was giving back to my community. As a prosecutor I was making an impact on the families who had lost loved ones to violence. I seemed to be giving them some measure of comfort in knowing that the person who had brought the sorrow and pain to their lives would be held accountable. It felt good. Despite the horrific nature of what had been inflicted on them, I was able to help in some small way. I liked what I was doing.

When I was assigned a new case, I'd schedule a meeting with the victims of the crime, or in the case of a homicide, the surviving family members. We'd discuss how their case would proceed through the court system, whether we might offer a plea, and what trial would be like if it came to that. Victims would give me their thoughts about a plea or whether they'd like to see the case proceed to a jury trial. While the final decision rests with the prosecutor, getting the victims' input and coming to a mutual decision, if possible, always made everyone feel a little better.

Within a short time in the county attorney's office, I was pretty much just trying homicide cases. Meeting with the surviving family members early on was emotional. The pain of having lost a loved one was usually still raw, and I often wondered how much of what I was explaining was actually being understood. It didn't take long before I realized that periodic meetings were necessary to repeat explanations of the case progress and trial prospects. My office had long had a victim services component, and victim advocates were assigned to all homicide cases. The advocates were invaluable. Their counseling and consultation with the victims took much of the load off the prosecutor, and the advocates would act as a go-between with the family and the prosecutor. With the advocates' help, meeting with victims' families became one of the most important and meaningful parts of the job. But with respect to the death penalty, it raised issues as well.

The loved ones of a murder victim had usually not thought

much about the death penalty until the violence of a killing was inflicted on their family. Then it was often brought up in my initial meeting with them. While it was never something I planned on discussing in the first meeting, some families wanted to know if the accused murderer would face the death penalty. Understandably some families thought the murderer should suffer the same fate as their loved one. It was often my job to explain to the family that the law simply didn't call for the state to seek that penalty in the death of their family member. It was often a difficult task.

There were times when families had given a lot of thought to the potential sentence, however. Many years ago I took a case of a double homicide involving the murder of two coeds at the university. Roommates, the young women had been shot multiple times during a burglary of their off-campus duplex. Both died. It was, I felt, the type of case where the suspects should face the death penalty. One of the victims I mentioned earlier had been the campus president of Amnesty International and was very much opposed to the death penalty. Her parents and brother explained to me how they did not wish the state to seek the death penalty in her name. They were calm but insistent.

Like with the families that insisted we seek death for the loss of their loved ones, I had to explain that while the family had input, the final decision was, and had to be, made by the prosecution based on all the factors of the case and the law. Just as I could not let one family dictate that we would file a death notice when they felt it was deserved, I couldn't let the family opposed to the death penalty make the final decision either. That was much harder, however. Who was I to subject the family to years of appeals and uncertainty by seeking a punishment to which they objected? I agonized at length about the decision. I concluded that the murders were much too cruel and senseless not to seek death.

Over the family's objection, I filed a death notice. Ultimately the main defendant was sentenced to life, and the other found not guilty. The family, having sat through the trials, felt it was the right outcome for both.

For over thirty years I've met with dozens of families after one of the worst things that could ever happen to them has happened. Tucson, although having a metropolitan population of over one million, is still a small town in many respects. I invariably run into some of these families over the years, and the sadness I first saw in their faces has never fully left. At times I've felt like seeing me in the grocery store or somewhere on the street has caused the pain of their loss to come flooding back, and I feel badly that I seem to reopen the wounds. But I came to realize that the wounds left with the surviving family members are always close to the surface.

When I see these families, we chat, bring each other up to date on our lives, and then go on our way. The initial meetings, trials and sentencings, and often long road of appeal can take an emotional toll on the prosecutor as well. It's difficult not to take the job home and discuss with your family not only the brutality of the cases but the emotional impact that the violence has left on surviving loved ones. It can give you quite a jaded view of people and what they are capable of doing to one another.

As hard as it is at times, a prosecutor has to keep some distance from the surviving family members. You aren't their lawyer but rather represent the state. I've seen prosecutors make the mistake of getting too close to the family members of a victim, being invited to and attending family functions for example. The distance, although seemingly cold, is important so that the decisions you make are based on the law and evidence and not what might be best or easier for the victims.

I've made the mistake myself. Once I gave the family of a murder victim my private cell phone number. The father and husband of this family had been a victim of a random carjacking and murder. The family was devastated and confused and, as the case went on, naturally had numerous questions. Although we'd met in my office several times, the widow especially was having a hard time retaining information, as she was so distraught. She began calling me at night and on weekends asking questions. As with many cases, something would be reported in the local paper about the case, and the article would occasionally contain faulty information. That would cause late-night calls to explain why the article differed from what I'd told them or what had happened in court. I learned to have folks only call my office phone. While I certainly wanted the families to have correct information, it was important to separate work and home life.

I found that separating work life and private life wasn't so easy. The job, to a large extent, defined who I was. My own family lived it, with my children knowing more about murder than any child should as they were growing up. Trials often involved working late into the night at home and on weekends to prepare. When I was more of a runner, I'd practice my closing arguments in my head as I ran at night through the university. The job can consume your life. But it's a job I've never wanted to trade for any other.

Over these years, I have met many remarkable and resilient people in my job. They were the surviving family members of loved ones who had been taken by violence. They were remarkable in that, in spite of the tragedy they suffered, they carried on in life and gave comfort to one another and bravely faced the court battles ahead of them. They were resilient in that, despite the ordeal of the investigation, the court hearings, and the often lengthy trials, they not only attended each hearing and the trials, but very often they provided me with the support I needed to continue. Seeing the family in court during trial always provided extra motivation to make sure justice was done. This book is to honor the courage that each of them showed and to honor the memory of their loved ones. I hope it does that.

SANDY

On March 11, 1980, Sandra Owen left the apartment on the east side of Tucson that she shared with a roommate to go to a mental health clinic and then to a local food stamp office in an attempt to speed up that application process. Sandy, as her family called her, was never seen alive again. She had just turned twenty-nine. Her roommate reported to the police that Sandy usually got around by hitchhiking the streets of Tucson. While this was her frequent method of getting from one place to another, on March 11, it led to her murder.

In February 1980, Kathy Foreman left the small East Texas city of Orange with two men, both older than her eighteen years. Joe Lambright, thirty-two at the time, had served a short stint in Vietnam and had returned home to his family in Texas, holding odd jobs and getting in trouble. Robert Smith, also thirty-two, lived nearby, holding various odd jobs as well. The three of them left Orange to see the country. First driving to Florida and then back to Orange, they dropped off another man who had made part

1

of the trip with them. The three then headed west through Texas to see California.

Foreman and Lambright had taken up with each other before they left Orange the first time, both of them leaving other partners to be together. Smith was traveling unaccompanied. As they headed west, the three would stop in small towns, picking up odd jobs for a day or two to earn money to keep them in gas and food. On March 10, 1980, they reached Tucson and decided to camp in some hills overlooking the city.

During the drive to Arizona, Lambright and Foreman frequently had sex in front of Smith. By the time they'd reached Arizona, Smith was tired of it and announced while camping that he needed a girl to have sex with. The next morning the three went to a coffee shop where Smith again told the others he needed a woman for sex. Foreman later reported to law enforcement that Lambright replied that they'd find one for him, stating further that he'd like to kill somebody "just to see if he could do it." It was now March 11, 1980.

Sandy was hitchhiking from the area around the University of Arizona, trying to get to the food stamp office on the east side. Lambright, Smith, and Foreman drove past her at Campbell and Speedway just outside the university and stopped to pick her up. Foreman later identified Sandy's picture from a police constructed photo lineup as the woman who had gotten into their car. Sandy asked to be taken to the food stamp office, according to Foreman, and Lambright, driving the car, headed east with Sandy's directions.

Once they arrived at the food stamp office, Foreman reported that Lambright drove to the back of the building and jumped into the back seat where Sandy was. Lambright told Sandy to keep quiet and she wouldn't get hurt. Smith got into the driver's seat, drove to the freeway, and turned toward Phoenix. Sandy, according to Foreman, sat scared and trembling.

———•———

On the freeway Lambright began to search Sandy's purse, and Sandy asked to sing a song to calm her nerves. North of the city, Smith pulled over in a desert area to allow Sandy to go to the bathroom. Lambright made her take her shoes off first so she couldn't run away. When Sandy returned to the car, Smith got into the back seat, and Lambright then continued to drive westbound. Smith covered the side and back windows with blankets and shirts and raped Sandy in the back seat of the car. Lambright and Smith told Sandy they'd let her go and take her back to where they had picked her up on Speedway. They didn't.

Lambright continued driving on the freeway, turning off several miles up the highway and heading onto a road leading to some mountains to the west. According to Foreman, it was getting late in the afternoon, and Lambright took a turn toward a mountain until the road was unusable. They got out and made Sandy walk up the side of the hill, where Foreman said they could see no buildings, houses, or other people.

On a flat area of the side of a desert mountain, far from anyone, far from her home, Sandy was raped again by Smith. Although they had promised to release her, clearly it was never in the minds of the two men. After this second rape, Smith began to choke Sandy, his arm tightening around her throat. Lambright grabbed a knife that Foreman carried on her belt and rushed to Sandy. Lambright, according to Foreman's later testimony, began stabbing Sandy and turning the knife inside of her body while she was held tightly by Smith. She described how Lambright slashed and hacked at Sandy's neck. As Sandy lay bleeding on this flat spot of land, Lambright picked up a large rock and smashed it down on her head. The three walked back down the hill to the car and drove away, leaving Sandy to die alone. Foreman would later tell the jury that the two men sang "We Are the Champions" out loud as they drove away.

While Sandy was reported missing by her mother, the remoteness of the scene prevented anyone from finding her body. In the meantime, Lambright, Smith, and Foreman returned to Orange, Texas. Sandy's body, over the course of a year in the desert heat and exposure, was reduced to skeletal remains.

As often happens in unsolved cases, the perpetrators eventually talk. I had prosecuted many cases in which days, weeks, or months after the murder, the killer told someone about it, unable to keep the details inside them any longer. Lambright's ex-wife, a victim of his physical abuse during their marriage, talked to a police officer in a small town in Louisiana, across the state line from Orange. She described how Lambright had detailed to her the killing of a woman in Tucson. That the victim had been repeatedly raped by Smith and then killed by Lambright with the assistance of Foreman. The ex-wife had kept this information to herself for months, only coming forward in early 1981.

Now with the names of all three suspects, police in Orange located Foreman and questioned her. Foreman gave it all up. She described how Sandy was picked up hitchhiking so that Smith "could have a woman." Foreman detailed Sandy's rape, forced march up the side of a mountain, and gruesome stabbing. She told police that not only did Lambright stab her but that he "wallowed" the knife around inside of Sandy.

———————

Police in Tucson were contacted about a potential victim by the name of Sandy who Foreman was now reporting she witnessed being murdered. Within hours that information led to a year-old missing persons report made by Sandy's mother. But still, there was no body.

Homicide detective Gary Dhaemers of the Pima County Sheriff's Office in Tucson decided to head to Texas to speak with Foreman. Once Dhaemers arrived and spoke to Foreman, she agreed to return to Tucson to try and find where Sandy had been left twelve months prior. Foreman gave a complete statement, detailing her involvement and the acts of Lambright and Smith. She spent days with Dhaemers and other detectives scouring the desert north of Tucson. By pure happenstance, while detectives were out trying to find the spot, a hunter came upon Sandy's remains. A year and six days after being murdered, Sandy was found.

Within a matter of days, Dhaemers and other detectives were back in Orange and with the help of local police quickly found both Smith and Lambright, who were still living there. Smith quickly confessed, though he minimized his own involvement, blaming most of the violent acts on Foreman and Lambright. Smith claimed that Sandy willingly participated in sex with him and that he only strangled her to render her unconscious to save her from the other two. But, he claimed, while he attempted to strangle her into unconsciousness, Lambright and Foreman repeatedly stabbed Sandy and cut her throat.

Lambright gave a bizarre account of Sandy's murder. While he agreed with most of Foreman's statement about picking up Sandy hitchhiking, Smith's repeated rapes of her, and the hike up a remote mountain, he feigned confusion as to the murder. He told detectives that Smith began to strangle Sandy and that all he could remember was seeing Smith and Foreman hold her arms down and "a knife being used." He refused to say who stabbed her, only that the three of them walked back down the mountain and drove to California. While he was being questioned, a distinctive star-shaped necklace was found on Lambright. Sandy's mom later identified it as one that Sandy wore all the time.

It was a year later, March 1982, when prosecutor Jim Himelic tried both men in front of separate juries, using Foreman as a witness. Himelic presented the terror unleashed on Sandy in the desert. A pathologist testified that the skeletal remains revealed repeated hacking to the front of the vertebrae of Sandy's neck, showing her neck was cut to the backbone. It took little time for either jury to convict the men of first-degree murder, kidnapping, and sexual assault.

Two months later, on May 27, 1982, two years and two months after Sandy's murder, the trial judge sentenced both men to death, calling the murder cold and calculated, the work of an abandoned and malignant heart. It would be thirty-four more years until the case was finally settled.

Death penalty cases, to state the obvious, take a long time. Not just to get them to trial but to wind their way through appellate review. While the time varies in different parts of the country depending on which federal circuit your state is located in, it takes years of one court after another to review the case. That's not a bad thing. Someone who is sentenced to death obviously deserves a thorough review of the evidence used against him, the fairness of the trial, the effectiveness of his attorney, the conduct of the prosecutor, and the fair application of the law by the trial judge. In the 9th Circuit US Court of Appeals, in which Arizona is located, that process often takes decades.

Once a defendant is sentenced to death, the case takes a somewhat meandering path through the judicial system. There is a direct appeal to the state supreme court. If the case survives there, it typically goes back to the trial court for a review of the fairness of the trial. While those steps can take three to five years, if the conviction and sentence are upheld in state court, the appeal proceeds into federal district court. This isn't intended to be even a primer on the federal appellate process, so suffice it to say that once a case enters the federal appeals path, especially in the 9th Circuit, the legal review of the case can proceed for twenty or even thirty years. Such was the case with both Smith and Lambright.

Between the two men and the appeals brought on their behalf by court-appointed lawyers, there are approximately fifty reported case decisions from various appellate courts from the 1980s through 2010. Keep in mind that at each step of the appeals process, a defendant is represented by a court-appointed attorney, often more than one. By any account, the cost of such appeals easily extends into the millions of dollars of both state and federal money for each capital defendant. Whether that cost to the taxpayer is worth it is certainly subject to much debate. But I think one has to look at the results of those cases to make that determination.

In November 2015, Joe Lambright was once again in front of a jury for the murder of Sandy Owen. Thirty-five years after killing her and having spent nearly thirty-four years on death row appealing his conviction and sentence, the 9th Circuit Court of Appeals mandated that Lambright should have a jury decide what his fate should be. After decades in the appeals system, the court finally concluded that Lambright's original trial lawyers at the 1982 trial did an insufficient job of defending him during his sentencing process. The court decided that the original defense lawyers should have presented much more evidence at the sentencing regarding Lambright's childhood trauma and his mental health issues. Because they failed to do so, the court concluded he should be resentenced.

In the intervening years, the law had changed regarding sentencing proceedings in capital cases. Prior to 2002, judges in several states, including Arizona, were the ones who made the decision. The US Supreme Court decided that year that only juries could render a verdict resulting in a death sentence. This ruling caused many cases to have resentencing trials where juries, not judges, would decide a murderer's fate. Going forward, any death penalty could only be imposed by a jury, and the decision, at least in Arizona, could not be changed by the judge.

Lambright was assigned new attorneys for sentencing. In Arizona the law requires two lawyers be appointed to represent an indigent defendant. In addition, investigators, mitigation specialists who investigate a defendant's background, family history, schooling, and many other aspects of the defendant's life, are also appointed. Expert witnesses such as psychologists and psychiatrists are also provided. It is extremely rare that a defendant has the funds to pay for any of this. Less than 1 percent of capital defendants can afford their own defense. The financial burden once again falls to the taxpayer.

———————

Seeing Lambright in court in 2015, I was struck by how small and frail he seemed. He'd spent three decades on death row, and while now only in his mid-sixties, he was not the person he was in 1980. The defense would focus on that for the new trial.

After thirty-five years, most of the witnesses in Sandy's murder had died. Foreman, the officers in Texas and Louisiana, the pathologist, the prosecutor and most of the other participants in the original trial were no longer alive. The jury would hear most of the testimony by having trial transcripts read to them. Their task was not to decide guilt, they were told that a jury in 1982 had already decided that issue. The job of this jury was to decide, without knowing why it was necessary thirty-three years after the last sentencing, what the appropriate sentence was for Sandy's murder. And, they were not told what the original sentence was. My co-counsel and I presented the facts of the murder mainly through previous testimony and the testimony of former detective Dhaemers, who had long since retired from law enforcement.

The defense presented mental health experts who testified that, in their opinion, Lambright left Vietnam a changed man. They stated that he suffered from post-traumatic stress at the time of the murder and argued the jury should take that into account in their decision. In addition, the defense brought in prison guards to say that for over three decades Lambright had been a model prisoner. While the jury knew he'd been in prison, they were not told Lambright had spent his time on death row. They were informed of his physical ailments, mainly common issues related to most men in their late sixties.

After several weeks of hearing evidence about the crime, Lambright's mental and physical health, his life story, and his upbringing and schooling, the jury went out to deliberate. After several days the jury informed the court they were deadlocked with half voting for the death penalty and half for life. The court declared a mistrial with the hung jury. It was then up to the prosecution to decide the next step.

In Arizona, after a hung jury on the sentencing issue, the law allows prosecutors to seek another trial with a new jury. With such a decision, the sentencing would start anew. New jurors would be impaneled, not being given any information about past sentences or attempts to seek death. We could have taken another shot at getting a death sentence. Sandy's sister, Janet, had come from out of state to watch the sentencing trial. After consulting with her and explaining that another trial might well have the same result, we made the decision not to ask for another trial.

There was no agreement with the defense. I simply told the judge and the defense lawyers that we were not asking for another trial and that we were withdrawing our notice to seek the death penalty. The sentencing decision would be left up to the judge.

In January of 2016, almost thirty-six years after the murder, nearly thirty-four years after being sentenced to death, Lambright was sentenced to spend another twenty years in prison. He would be eighty-seven if he serves that time. He is now appealing the judge's sentence, claiming he should be out of prison.

Robert Smith's case took a somewhat different turn. In 2002, along with deciding that only a jury could determine whether a death sentence was appropriate, the US Supreme Court decided in a separate case that it was unconstitutional to execute someone who was mentally retarded, now referred to as intellectually disabled. Smith had followed much the same path as Lambright in filing his appeals and up until 2002 had not succeeded in getting relief. But after the new holding by the Supreme Court, Smith's lawyers filed motions that he was indeed intellectually disabled, essentially that he suffered from extremely low intelligence and that his adaptive behavior, that is, his inability to take care of himself, rendered him legally ineligible to be executed. Thus began a several-year court contest on whether Robert Smith had been unconstitutionally on death row for over twenty years. It was not a short battle.

Once again experts were retained on both sides to evaluate Smith, his intelligence, his level of functioning, and whether he met the statutory definition of someone who was intellectually disabled. After a lengthy hearing in 2007, at which numerous mental health experts testified about Smith's level of functioning, the trial judge determined that Smith's claim of intellectual disability was unfounded and so ordered in 2008. The testimony from experts on both sides was that Smith's IQ was in the nineties, well above the statutory range for someone with intellectual disability and in the low-normal range of the general population. The judge's conclusions were upheld by the Arizona Court of Appeals, the Arizona Supreme Court, and then the US District Court over the ensuing years of appeals. But then Smith's case made it back to the 9th Circuit Court of Appeals. Eight years later, in 2016, that court disagreed.

Instead of relying on the testimony of the experts who testified in court in 2007, the circuit court cited to a school test administered to Smith in 1964. A judge dissenting from the majority summed it up best:

In 1964, when Smith was 15, he took the Otis IQ test and received scores of 62 and 71. The state court found that the "Otis test was developed in approximately the 1920s and was outmoded at the time it was reportedly given to (Smith) in 1964." More importantly, "there is no evidence concerning the qualifications of the persons administering the tests, whether an appropriate protocol was followed, the specific circumstances of (Smith) at the times of the tests, or any of the other information required to determine the validity of these school record entries."

In short, despite the lower court listening to testimony that Smith was in the normal range of IQ and functioning based on testimony from both state and defense experts, and despite several intermediate courts upholding that trial judge's findings, the 9th Circuit focused on an outdated school test given over forty years prior with little information regarding who administered the test or under what circumstances and ruled that Smith was indeed intellectually disabled. Given the 2002 Supreme Court ruling, Smith was not eligible for a death sentence and could not be retried, so the court ordered that he be sentenced to life. In late 2016 he was. He also will be eligible for parole when he is eighty-seven should he still be alive. He also is appealing his new sentence and is arguing that he should be released from prison now.

While it's easy to cast blame on the "system" or the courts or even the prosecution, this is not a unique outcome with capital cases. If you support and believe in a death penalty system, it's difficult to find many murders more deserving of the ultimate punishment. Sandy's killing was senseless and cruel. But Lambright and Smith escaped the death sentence. The end of the three decades of litigation could just as easily have gone against both men and upheld their original sentences. A different set of judges hearing the appeals may have come to different conclusions.

Sandy's murder in 1980 was horrific. She was frightened and alone. She was repeatedly raped and undoubtedly suffered physically and emotionally. She was stabbed and choked, and her throat was sliced by Lambright while she was being held by Smith. She was left alone to die on top of a mountain miles from anyone. There was no question as to the identity of her killers. But thirty-four years after first being sentenced to death, after countless sums of money being spent on their many appeals during those decades, both men are off death row and are still, for now, behind prison walls.

SUSAN, ANNA, AND GABRIEL

On February 2, 1984, I was the duty attorney of the day, tasked with attending initial appearances. There I saw anyone arrested for a felony in Pima County in the previous twenty-four hours brought before a judge to have conditions of release decided and to appoint an attorney. My job was to make bail recommendations on behalf of the state for anyone I felt might be a flight risk or could be too dangerous to release. It's a rather boring task, as you sit in court for two to three hours watching one suspect after another being brought in to seek release pending trial. That day was the first time I saw James Granvil Wallace. I could not guess then that twenty years later I would be spending several years seeking the death penalty against him for the charges he was being seen for that day.

When James Wallace was brought into court for his initial appearance, I knew he was not someone I would easily forget. Most suspects coming into court are relatively calm, knowing that a good impression might help the judge impose a low bond or even release without bail. Wallace was different. He was crying and sobbing, telling the judge and everyone in court that he was guilty, that he had killed three people and that he needed to die. It is common for convicted defendants to express remorse for their crimes before they are sentenced. Many times it is hard not to roll your eyes because you've heard claims of remorse over and over. Early in your career in criminal law, you reach a healthy skepticism when you hear a defendant claim how sorry he is for the crime he committed. Wallace was clearly different. With good reason.

Even though I'd only been a prosecutor less than three years at the time, I had no doubt this man was expressing true remorse. Between the sobs, there was truly an aspect to his pleas to the judge that made it clear he was horrified at what he had done. There was no reason to doubt that he wanted someone to kill him right at that moment. The day before, he had beaten to death Susan Insalaco and her two children, Anna, age sixteen, and Gabriel, age twelve. These murders led to the imposition of the death penalty for Wallace four separate times.

Two nights before, on January 31, 1984, Wallace was at the home he shared with Susan and her children. Susan and Wallace had lived together about two years while she worked, raised Anna and Gabe, and put up with Wallace's drinking and pot use. The night of January 31, Susan had finally had enough. While she held down a steady job, Wallace had worked on and off and brought little money in to support the household. Wallace had left his own family behind in Colorado some years before, walking away from a job, a wife, and a child and found himself in Tucson, where he met Susan. They began living together in a small home on the northwest side of the city.

On January 31, Susan told Wallace that he needed to leave the next day. She could no longer tolerate his drinking, drug use, and failure to hold a job, and she had her children to consider.

Susan told Wallace that he needed to pack up his things and be gone before the children got home from school the next afternoon around three o'clock. Susan left for work the morning of February 1, leaving Wallace alone in the house. Rather than pack up, he sat at the house drinking beer and bourbon and smoking marijuana for most of the day. Anna was the first to arrive home.

———•—•———

Most murders are senseless to some degree. Greed is a motive for some, uncontrollable anger for others, and sometimes it is for revenge. I think we try hard to ascribe some motive for a murder, in part because we need it to have a rational basis, and, in part, to convince ourselves it couldn't happen to us. There are times you get a murder that defies any explanation. You simply can't imagine it, and hard as you might try, you can't come up with a motive. It's tempting to say that some people are just evil. But that doesn't satisfy the desire to put a reason to the violence that some people inflict.

Anna arrived home from school at quarter till three in the afternoon. Wallace was waiting for her behind the front door. He had armed himself with a baseball bat. Not a full-size one, but a souvenir bat you can buy at professional baseball games. It was a solid piece of wood. As Anna stepped into the house, Wallace began beating her in the back of her head with the bat. Over and over he slammed the bat onto her skull. Later, a pathologist would say that he couldn't count the exact number of blows inflicted. The injuries to Anna's head overlapped, one skull fracture running into another, and made any accurate number of injuries impossible to determine. Maybe fifteen. Maybe twenty.

But Anna didn't die. After repeated strikes with the bat, it broke, the handle now sharp and jagged. Anna had fallen to the floor but was still breathing. Wallace knew Gabe would be arriving home soon, so he dragged Anna's body down the hall to a back bathroom. He could hear her moans and labored breathing. With the broken bat still in his hand, Wallace pointed the now sharpened end toward Anna's throat. He thrust the bat into her neck with such force the jagged end hit the floor beneath her, embedding a necklace with a small cross into her throat. Wallace closed the bathroom door and looked for another weapon.

Before twelve-year-old Gabe got home, Wallace had time to rush to the backyard and open the shed. There he picked up an eighteen-inch pipe wrench. It was a heavy, solid piece of steel. He again waited behind the front door. Gabe got home from school just after three o'clock. It had taken Wallace only fifteen minutes to beat Anna to death, drag her from sight, and arm himself again. Gabe entered the house and saw Wallace, asking him why he was still at the house after Susan had told him to leave. Wallace followed Gabe toward his bedroom, the wrench in his hand.

As Gabe entered his room, Wallace, as he had done only minutes before with Anna, began violently striking the young boy with the wrench. Repeatedly using the heavy steel to strike Gabe's head, Wallace hit him with such force that Gabe's brain was extruded onto the floor of the bedroom. The violence inflicted was unimaginable. Once again the pathologist could only guess at the number of blows. Maybe twelve. Maybe fifteen. They all merged together.

Now Wallace had nearly two hours before Susan would arrive home from work. Anna and Gabe lay dead in separate rooms but only a few feet apart. Wallace left them where they were and waited for Susan, wrench in hand. While waiting, Wallace got a small-caliber handgun out of his bedroom and loaded it. He thought about shooting himself, and he thought about using it on Susan. He discarded both ideas, realizing the gunshots could attract attention from neighbors.

Shortly after five o'clock Susan walked into the house carrying groceries toward the kitchen. She saw Wallace and undoubtedly had only a few seconds to try to understand what was happening. Anna and Gabe's bodies lay at the other side of the house from the kitchen, but Susan had to have wondered where they were, why they hadn't come out to greet her, especially since Wallace was standing in front of her. She didn't have long to consider the situation.

Once Susan had set the groceries on the kitchen counter, Wallace raised the wrench. As he had with Anna, as he had with Gabe, Wallace began beating Susan in the head. She made it a few steps into the dining room before she fell to the floor, dead from four to five blows to the head with the same wrench that had killed her son. The house now quiet, Wallace opened Susan's purse that she'd placed on the kitchen counter. Inside he found ten dollars and put it in his pocket. He walked outside and closed the door.

At a liquor store, Wallace bought some beer and called a friend, asking if he could spend the night since Susan had kicked him out. Wallace took the beer to the friend's house and spent the evening playing chess and drinking beer with his friend. He made no mention of what had happened. The next morning when he awoke, Wallace told his friend that he had killed Susan and the children. The friend called the police and handed the phone to Wallace, who explained what he had done. Wallace told them to go to Susan's house and they would find the bodies of the three people he had murdered.

While some officers responded to Susan's home, others went to the home where Wallace had spent the night. They found Wallace outside near the street waiting for them. He was taken down to the station and questioned while detectives began viewing the carnage left behind at Susan's. There was no holding back. Wallace described in detail what he had done to Anna, Gabe, and then Susan. He described how surprised he was that it took so many blows to kill a person. He had no explanation for the murders of Anna or Gabe, and when asked why he killed Susan, he only replied, "Because I killed the children."

As he would several hours later when I saw him in court, Wallace cried in front of the detectives who questioned him. He begged them to take him out behind the station and shoot him because he didn't want to live. He explained that once they saw what he had done, they would understand why he should just be shot. It was a horrific scene. Detectives took hours collecting evidence at Susan's house, recovering the bodies, the wrench, the broken bat. It would be the worst day most of the officers would ever have.

Wallace was appointed an attorney to defend him, but putting up a defense never seemed to be in Wallace's plans. A more senior prosecutor was assigned this triple murder as I was, at that time, a fairly new attorney. After a year of litigation regarding the admissibility of the evidence against him, and against the advice of his attorney, Wallace pled guilty to all charges on March 1, 1985. There was no plea agreement and no stipulation regarding sentencing. His attorney had Wallace evaluated by a psychologist, which showed that he was mentally competent, that he understood the proceedings, and that he was legally able to enter a plea of guilty. The defense attorney filed a memorandum with the court stating that his client had desired for months to plead guilty and asked the court to appoint another mental health expert for sentencing. The court did so.

On May 10, 1985, the court heard from experts, police officers, and lay witnesses about the defendant's mental health, his remorse, and his background. On May 15, Judge James Carruth was set to impose sentence. As seasoned and experienced as Judge Carruth was, the murders of Anna, Gabe, and Susan had to be the worst he'd seen in his years on the bench. The US Supreme Court was still seventeen years away from deciding that judges alone could not impose a death sentence and that only juries could make that decision. So, the decision as to penalty fell to Carruth. He found genuine remorse on the part of Wallace to be a mitigating factor, but he could not overlook the horror of the murders.

The law in Arizona in 1984 had very few statutory aggravating factors. These are findings that a judge, now a jury, has to make in addition to the verdict for the crime of first-degree murder. In other words, not every murder is subject to the death penalty. The US Supreme Court has said that the death penalty should be reserved for the "worst of the worst" of murderers. The law requires an additional finding beyond the murder to elevate it to a capital case. For Wallace the only aggravating factor was that the murders were found to be "cruel, heinous or depraved."

While we all might have in our minds what those terms mean, over the years the Arizona Supreme Court has defined each of those words in legal terms. Based on the nature of the murders, Judge Carruth agreed that they were inflicted in a cruel, heinous, or depraved manner and imposed the death sentence for each of the three murders.

It would be twenty-seven years and three more sentencing hearings before the case would be closed and the court would decide Wallace should receive a life sentence. The court arrived at that conclusion in 2012 only after taking a circuitous route of appeals, lengthy jury trials on sentencing, and four separate opinions by the Arizona Supreme Court. If anyone belonged on death row, it was James Wallace. Yet twenty-eight years after the most horrific murders one can imagine, the court found that he was not death eligible.

In Arizona, after the imposition of a death sentence, the case is automatically appealed to the state supreme court. In the 1980s, the court conducted an independent review of the appropriateness of the death penalty being imposed. If the court determined that the defendant was not one of the "worst of the worst," it could make a finding that the death penalty was not legally supported. Such a review was held in 1986 in what became known as Wallace I.

In this first appeal, the court found the facts of the murders to meet the legal standard of heinousness and depravity. The court called the killings "brutal" for the repeated blows to the heads of the victims. Wallace was found to have inflicted "gratuitous violence" for shoving the jagged portion of the baseball bat through Anna's throat. The opinion noted that had Wallace merely intended to kill, he had a less violent means available to carry out the killings with the loaded gun. But because he chose not to use it, the court stated that Wallace's conduct reflected a "total disregard for human life."

The court further found that not only were the murders senseless but that by lying in wait for hours, these brutal killings were "particularly disturbing." The Arizona Supreme Court had heard a lot of murder cases, but this one stood out. The court concluded its opinion by stating these senseless and gruesome murders certainly justified the sentences imposed. The holding affirmed the findings of Judge Carruth and the sentences with respect to Anna and Gabe. Finding a technical flaw in Carruth's sentence for Susan's death, the court ordered the judge to hold a new hearing on Susan's murder. In all other respects, the imposed sentences would stand. In August 1987, Judge Carruth once again heard from numerous mental health experts, lay witnesses, medical doctors, and detectives. Once again finding the murder of Susan to be heinous and depraved, the judge imposed the death sentence.

Because all death sentences are automatically appealed to the state supreme court, Wallace was back on appeal. In 1989 the Arizona Supreme Court, in a brief opinion, Wallace II, recited the facts of the murders once again. As they had three years prior, the court found the murder of Susan to be senseless, particularly disturbing, heinous, and depraved. The death sentence, the court held then, was justified. Judge Carruth was tasked with hearing additional matters related to the effectiveness of Wallace's defense attorney, new allegations about his mental health, and the appropriateness of the death sentences. Those were denied, and Wallace's appeals then proceeded into federal court and into the hands of the 9th Circuit Court of Appeals.

Over the next decade, Wallace's case was litigated in federal court. While it may seem odd to anyone other than a lawyer, the federal courts review the same issues that have been extensively litigated in the state courts to determine whether any federal constitutional protections have been violated. It's not only a long process, but new lawyers are appointed, often new experts are retained, and federal judges review the case to decide whether the sentence should be upheld or sent back to state court to do it all again. In the 9th Circuit, it is often the latter.

First, a case proceeds to the federal district court. This is the trial level of the federal system, but the federal judge assigned has the power to grant relief to a state death row inmate and order the state court to conduct new hearings. Here, the district court judge denied relief to Wallace, refusing his claim that his lawyers rendered ineffective assistance at sentencing. After all, multiple mental health experts testified in state court regarding Wallace's mental state, along with numerous other witnesses. The district court judge declined to order a new state hearing on punishment.

Wallace appealed that ruling to the 9th Circuit. In 1999, that court reversed the holding of the federal district judge and ordered the case back for additional hearings. The 9th Circuit, in looking at the same facts that every other judge had seen, found that the "bizarre circumstances of the crime suggest that Wallace may have been acting as a result of some mental infirmity," yet he was "nevertheless sentenced to death." Just like the rest of us, the 9th Circuit wanted there to be a motive for these murders that they could put a label on. It was too awful otherwise. Even though several mental health experts had testified at sentencing and numerous psychological tests given to Wallace by these doctors, it was all insufficient for the federal appellate court. Wallace was getting a new sentencing hearing. In late 2002, the district court judge who had initially declined to give Wallace relief followed the mandate of the court of appeals and ordered Wallace's case back into state court.

In early 2002, the US Supreme Court in a case called *Ring v. Arizona* had ruled that only juries could decide the issue of the imposition of the death penalty and not judges alone, so for the first time, Wallace was going to have his case heard by a jury. On December 9, 2002, almost nineteen years after seeing him crying at his initial appearance, I had Wallace brought into the courtroom of Judge Virginia Kelly. The prosecution had to decide whether to seek the death penalty again after such a long time or allow Judge Kelly to impose life sentences. A month later, in January 2003, and after consulting the victims' family about sitting through everything again, we notified the judge and the new defense attorneys that the state would again seek the death penalty.

Over the course of the next two years, Wallace was assigned an entirely new defense team. The attorneys appointed in December 2002 stated they couldn't be ready in any reasonable amount of time, and Judge Kelly, a no-nonsense jurist, replaced them. In addition, at county expense, Wallace's attorneys were able to hire a team of investigators, psychologists, and a mitigation specialist. In 2005, we were finally ready to pick a jury for a several-week trial, informing them that they were not sitting to decide guilt but rather to decide whether Wallace should be put to death for his crimes.

Over five weeks of trial, the jury heard gruesome details regarding the crime. They were not told about the previous sentences of death or any of the findings of the various courts. The jury was told that Wallace had pled guilty to the murders and that, despite the lengthy passage of time from 1985 when that occurred, they were to render sentence. The defense once again presented witnesses in court. Mental health experts, family members, and evidence of his background and upbringing were heard by the jury.

The defense experts focused on Wallace's youth. In murder cases I'm never surprised about evidence of a defendant's upbringing. Some cases are truly bizarre. Wallace's was perhaps not as bad as some that I've seen over the years, his family background was certainly different than most of ours. Wallace's mother suffered from her own mental problems. She would often hide for days or weeks somewhere in the house, coming out only when the rest of the family was asleep to get food. She would jump out of hiding places without any clothes on, scaring anyone who might be in the house. Alcohol and drug abuse was a large part of Wallace's childhood and carried over into his adulthood. Wallace's attempt at military service, his job history, and a family he'd left behind in Colorado were all issues the jury heard about from the defense experts, trying to paint a picture of a person scarred forever in youth and suffering from mental illness and drug and alcohol addiction.

As with the detectives who first discovered the bodies twenty-one years prior, this had to be the worst thing that the jurors had ever heard. They had to review the evidence, including the bat and wrench. The jury had to look at the photos of the crime scene and the bodies. They deliberated for seven hours and decided that Wallace was indeed one of the "worst of the worst." They imposed the death sentence for each of the three victims.

As in 1984, a sentence of death was automatically appealed to the Arizona Supreme Court. One of the issues before the sentencing trial was how to define the idea of heinousness and depravity to the jury. Judge Kelly had solicited ideas from both sides. I had suggested that we use the language the Supreme Court had used in Wallace I when the court had described why the brutality of the murders met the legal definition. It seemed reasonable. The Arizona Supreme Court disagreed.

The Supreme Court acknowledged that in Wallace I they found the murders to be heinous and depraved and that the court in that 1985 opinion saw the fact that Wallace could have used a gun rather than killing the victims by beating them supportive of that finding. But by the time of Wallace III in 2008, the Supreme Court had changed its view of the law. In citing to their own holding in another murder case earlier in 2008, three years *after* our 2005 trial, the Supreme Court ruled that the jury should have been given an instruction on heinousness and depravity that followed the court's current thinking. They reversed the death sentences and remanded the case for new trial. But, they said, because Susan had suffered only four or five blows to the head in rapid succession, her murder was not subject to the death penalty. Despite the court's own ruling in Wallace II, they ruled the murder of Susan was to be punished by the only other available sentence in 1984, life in prison with the possibility of parole after twenty-five years. Wallace had served twenty-four.

We were back in court. In 2009, we picked a new jury. They were not told anything of the history of the case on appeal, the previous sentences, or court rulings. They were to start fresh and were only told that Wallace had pled guilty to the murders of Anna and Gabe and the jury was to decide the appropriate sentence.

It should be noted that anywhere along the history of the case from 1984 until 2009 when the jury was being selected to hear the case again, the state has the authority to drop the request for the death penalty and seek life sentences. It was certainly discussed at length. Aside from the decades of appeals, we were most concerned about the effect of yet another trial recounting the murders on Susan's and the children's surviving family. It's hard to imagine the pain revisited on them every time we went to court. Ultimately everyone agreed, if Arizona was going to have a death penalty, James Wallace should receive it. So, we tried the case again.

The evidence was almost identical to that of the 2005 trial, of course. The state's facts didn't change, and the defense presented much the same by way of mental health experts, family background, and upbringing. After a four-week trial, the new jury deliberated a day, and for the fourth time in over twenty-five years of litigation, James Granvil Wallace was again sentenced to death. It was not the end.

———

As with his previous sentences, an automatic appeal went to the Arizona Supreme Court. Three years later, on March 26, 2012, the court rendered its opinion in Wallace IV. The opinion stated that "even among capital cases, this case is atrocious." The murders were, according to the court, senseless, and the unsuspecting victims were helpless and defenseless. But the court ruled it could not find that Wallace knew or should have known that he was inflicting more violence on the victims than was necessary to kill them. Although in Wallace I and II, the Arizona Supreme Court had made specific findings that the murders were legally heinous and depraved, in 2012 that court held this:

> *In common parlance, Wallace's crimes undoubtedly would be characterized as heinous or depraved. But under*

the Supreme Court's jurisprudence, we must apply narrowing constructions of those words, not the common understandings.

The court had simply changed its mind. Twenty-eight years after Wallace beat to death three innocent people, after being sentenced to die on four separate occasions over that time period, the Supreme Court ordered life sentences for the murders of Gabe and Anna to be served consecutively to the life sentence for the murder of Susan.

Wallace will undoubtedly die in prison. Not by the hands of the state in the execution chamber, but because of old age. The path from 1984 through 2012, especially given not only the certainty of Wallace's guilt but the horrific and senseless nature of the murders, has given me great pause regarding the continued use of the death penalty. As I noted above, if James Wallace does not deserve to be on death row and be executed by the state for his crimes, then who does? There are many others who remain on death row whose crimes, while horrible, don't rise to the level of atrocity of the murders of Susan and her children. Despite the effort, expense, and time that goes into prosecuting and defending these cases, the ultimate decision as to whether such a murderer lives or dies is, as the next case shows, dependent upon the "vagaries of the criminal justice system."

JENNIFER

On the morning of June 13, 1992, a jogger out in the early morning on the far east side of Tucson saw a car parked in the desert near his home. One door was open, and he saw no one around. Walking up to the car, he found the body of a young woman. She was lying in the dirt, one hand clutching some plant material broken from a nearby bush. Blood was everywhere.

When deputies arrived at the scene, they found eighteen-year-old Jennifer Geuder. She had been shot six times in the head. Her body was partially underneath her car, and the evidence and marks at the scene demonstrated that she had tried to scoot herself underneath it to escape the shooting. The desert floor underneath the car showed Jennifer had moved her legs and arms in a vain attempt to protect herself. The twigs in her hand showed she was grasping at anything within reach to shield herself. Nothing, and no one, protected her as she was left alone to die. Jennifer was the mother of a six-month-old baby boy.

When detectives notified her parents of the finding of Jennifer's body, they learned that she had gone out the night before, June 12, to meet her baby's father, her former boyfriend, and see a movie. Joe Anthony Luna was nineteen and had married another woman and was not supporting his child with Jennifer. Although Jennifer was living with her parents and raising her son, she had recently begun to seek child support from Luna. Jennifer had asked Luna to pay fifty dollars a month for diapers and formula to help her with expenses. Instead, Luna decided to kill her.

A couple days after Jennifer's body was found, a friend of Luna's came to police and told them that a few days before, Luna had asked the friend to help kill Jennifer. Luna described the plan and said another friend, Don Miller, would be helping also. The man who came forward told detectives that he declined to help, but he also did not do anything to warn Jennifer or anyone else what Luna had planned. After Jennifer was found, he did point detectives to Miller, and the police began looking for both him and Luna.

On June 15, 1992, armed with a search warrant, the SWAT team entered Miller's house and detained him. Detectives asked him to come with them to the station to answer some questions. Miller did. A surprising number of criminal defendants confess. Much is due to the skill of individual detectives, but I think much is also due to a person's need to confess the horror of what he has done. Miller confessed and told the detectives what he and Luna had done to Jennifer.

After picking Jennifer up and going to a movie, Miller said he, Luna, and Jennifer drove up Mt. Lemmon, a nearby mountain popular for hikes and drives. They took two vehicles, Jennifer's and Luna's, with Luna driving Jennifer's car and Miller following in Luna's. Stopping at a lookout point, Miller walked up to Jennifer's car as Luna pulled out a .25-caliber handgun that Miller had given him earlier in the evening. Luna shot Jennifer one time in the head, tossed the gun to Miller, and told him to follow him back down the mountain. Once down, Luna drove into a desert area close by.

———

Miller described to detectives how Jennifer was bleeding heavily and told them how he thought she might already be dead. Detectives, having been at the scene, knew this wasn't true, as they had witnessed what was clearly an attempt by Jennifer to escape. Miller then changed his story and said that he knew she was suffering and wanted to get her to a hospital. Instead, as Jennifer fought to hide herself under her car, Miller shot her five more times in the head. The two men drove away in Luna's car, leaving Jennifer bleeding and dying alone in the desert.

Luna had also been arrested by the police the same day as Miller. Rather than discuss anything about Jennifer, he claimed to know nothing about the murder. Detectives discovered that Luna's mother and wife had cleaned his car and bought four new tires to replace the ones that had left impressions in the dirt near Jennifer's body. They had already taken a statement from Luna's friend who'd stated that Luna had asked him to help kill Jennifer, but they had little other evidence, other than Miller's own confession, a statement that would be legally inadmissible at a trial against Luna.

Both men were arrested for first-degree murder and kidnapping and jailed. A month later I conducted a preliminary hearing. This is a sort of mini trial in front of a judge to establish that enough evidence exists to charge a defendant with a crime. Often prosecutors simply present a case to a grand jury for an easier and quicker hearing, but I wanted to make sure some testimony was preserved. Miller's two roommates had given statements to the detectives that Miller had come home from the shooting and confessed to them. Neither roommate was likely to be around for a trial or at least would be much less cooperative as the months went by before trial. In addition, Luna's friend who had told detectives about Luna's attempt to recruit him could also disappear before any trial. Calling them to testify at a preliminary hearing gave the defense a chance to cross-examine the witnesses and, importantly for me, preserve their testimony should they become unavailable.

Both Miller and Luna had been appointed lawyers who were very experienced and knew how to do their jobs. But after hearing from the witnesses and in light of Miller's confession, the judge had little trouble finding sufficient evidence to charge them both with the crimes for which they'd been arrested. In discussing the case with my colleagues, I had already decided to file a notice against both men that, in the event of a conviction for first-degree murder, the state would seek the death penalty. In another chapter I'll discuss how prosecutors make these decisions. But in 1992, a decade into my career, I had sole authority to file a notice that would bring about a sentence of death for a convicted murderer. It didn't take anyone's permission or review and didn't require a judge to approve of the filing. After the preliminary hearing, I filed a one-page document that made the case a capital murder.

From July 1992 until the spring of the following year, the case proceeded like any other. Motions to keep out Miller's confession and other evidence seized were filed and litigated. As Miller's confession would be legally inadmissible against Luna, the two would have to have separate trials. Then, in April of 1993, Luna's lawyer told me he would plead guilty to the murder and kidnapping if the death notice was withdrawn.

Some prosecutor's offices seem to believe it ethically appropriate to use the death penalty as a bargaining tool. In other words, if the prosecution files a death notice, that may prompt a defendant into pleading guilty just to avoid a possible death sentence. I'm of the firm belief that a prosecutor simply should not do that. If the decision has been made to seek death, then the case should proceed as such. My practice has been not to make any kind of plea offer once a death notice is filed. The intent is to proceed to trial. But when a defendant offers to plead guilty and accept a life sentence, you have to consider the alternatives.

As the evidence against Luna was weaker than it was against Miller, given his confession to the police and his roommates, I gathered up Jennifer's family to discuss the alternatives. Go to trial and try to seek the death penalty, or take Luna's offer and the sure conviction. While a legal decision for me, based on the facts and law, consider what Jennifer's parents were being asked to decide. They were in the process of adopting and raising Jennifer's child. The baby's mother was dead, and I was seeking to put the father to death. I couldn't put myself in their shoes well enough to realize the horrible decision they were being asked to make. We decided together to accept the defense offer. The man who planned the death, got Jennifer out of her house the night of June 12, and who shot her first would escape the death penalty.

From a factual perspective, it was clearly the best alternative for the state. While the evidence against Luna was pretty good, we faced the possibility of not being able to convict him at trial. But Luna, despite Miller shooting Jennifer five times, was morally the most culpable. He was the one who wanted Jennifer dead. On April 27, 1993, Luna entered his plea of guilty to both crimes. A month later, Judge Larry Fleischman imposed a life sentence for murder and a consecutive twenty-one years for kidnapping. At that time "life" in Arizona meant an inmate had to serve twenty-five calendar years before being eligible for parole. For Luna then, he'd serve twenty-five years and then be eligible to apply for parole to his consecutive sentence of another twenty-one. Under the law in effect at the time, he only has to serve fourteen of the twenty-one

years. If successful before the parole board, Luna would be fif-
ty-eight when he could be back on the streets.

After pleading Luna, who we felt was the more culpable, we
decided that Miller should be given the same option. I had to
ignore my position that once a death notice was filed, the case
would go to trial. Miller could plead guilty, take responsibility for
Jennifer's death, and escape the death penalty. He wanted us to
drop the kidnapping, but we refused. He decided to go to trial.
In July 1993, after a five-day trial, a jury convicted Miller of the
murder and kidnapping. It was an easy decision for them. Since
this was prior to the US Supreme Court decision in 2002 mandat-
ing jury decisions in death penalty sentencings, it was left to Judge
Fleischman to decide the sentence for Miller.

In order to impose a death sentence, a judge must find the existence of at least one statutory aggravating factor. That is, the court
must find evidence that the state has proved beyond a reasonable
doubt the evidence shows a circumstance beyond just the murder
itself. In Arizona these factors are such things as a prior serious
conviction, a prior murder, or killing multiple people at the same
time. In Miller's case I had alleged that the murder was especially
cruel, heinous, and depraved. This aggravating factor had been the
topic of many Arizona Supreme Court cases attempting to define
what those terms meant. They were legally elusive.

The cases, at least in the early 1990s, held that in order for
the state to prove this factor, the court had to find that the victim
consciously suffered and that the murderer inflicted gratuitous
violence. Judge Fleischman found that I had proven this by the fact
that Jennifer clearly struggled where she was shot five times, and
that after killing her Miller had yanked a large chunk of her hair
from her head, thus establishing gratuitous violence. The hair had
been found near Jennifer's body by detectives.

Once the aggravating factor is proven, it is the job of the

defense attorney to produce as much mitigation as he can find in an effort to save his client's life. Under the law, virtually anything regarding the defendant's character, background, upbringing, and history is admissible in an effort to avoid the death penalty. Miller's lawyers did their job.

Over the course of multiple days, the defense brought evidence from mental health experts, social workers, Miller's family members, and other attorneys who had represented him. They tried to show the judge that Miller had problems with alcohol brought on by an abusive childhood. They demonstrated that while he was not mentally ill, his family background and childhood abuse were factors that called for leniency. The main factor though, which I expected after pleading Luna, was that Miller should not be subject to the death penalty because the person most responsible had escaped death. It was, of course, a good argument.

Judge Fleischman was a very capable jurist. He'd spent a couple of decades doing criminal defense, mainly in appellate work. I knew from past experience that he was not in favor of the death penalty but would work very hard to enforce and follow the law. On December 20, 1993, he made his decision. He announced his decision in court with Jennifer's parents and brother present, along with several family friends. The judge went over each mitigating factor and how he had weighed it against the aggravating factor he'd found that I'd proven. Reaching under the bench where he sat, he pulled up the bag of hair pulled from Jennifer's head that had been admitted into evidence. Jennifer's mother reacted in horror at seeing her daughter's hair pulled up and exhibited. Had I known the judge was going to do this, I may have had time to dissuade him or at least prepare the victims. But it was this, Fleischman stated, that showed Miller's actions to be depraved and heinous.

As to the plea for Luna, Judge Fleischman was clearly troubled by the disparate treatment. Calling Luna one of the most despicable and cowardly individuals the judge had dealt with, Fleischman ruled that Luna's escaping of the death penalty was a factor that showed the "vagaries of the criminal justice system and the state of the evidence against him" but was not grounds for leniency. Miller was sentenced to death.

———

Less than three years later, in July 1996, the Arizona Supreme Court reviewed Miller's conviction and sentence. The court considered Judge Fleischman's rulings regarding the admissibility of the evidence, his trial rulings, and the sufficiency of the evidence. The court also considered the mitigation, taking note of Miller's background, childhood, and lack of any previous serious criminal activity. As to the plea accepted by Luna, the court simply stated that it was not mitigating. After this independent review, the Arizona Supreme Court affirmed Miller's conviction and death sentence.

Volunteers is a term prosecutors use in some death penalty cases that applies to inmates who no longer wish to appeal their death sentences. While it is a small portion of those convicted and sentenced to death, Miller was a volunteer. After his death sentence was affirmed by the court, Miller began a process of attempting to represent himself. As I previously discussed with Lambright's and Smith's cases, the appeal of a death sentence usually proceeds into federal court, where it is litigated for some years, even decades. I've had two cases where the defendants became volunteers.

Life on death row, as can be imagined, is unpleasant. In the years of Miller's incarceration, an inmate was isolated in a cell by himself and got brief periods of time in an outside enclosed area during the week. There were no contact visits like other inmates were provided. It is a life that some inmates can't bear. Miller was one of those. Although the first appeal after conviction to the state

supreme court is automatic, appeals afterward are not manda-
tory. While the vast majority of death row inmates take advantage
of every appeal available, a small number decide they want it to
end. By early 2000, Miller had successfully waived his remaining
appeals. A judge had to be satisfied that he was mentally competent
to do so, and two psychiatrists were appointed to evaluate him. The
court allowed Miller to withdraw all remaining avenues of appeal.

Executions, by law, must have witnesses. There are four groups.
The victim's family may attend, as well as the defendant's family.
The media are invited, and finally there is the official group, which
consists of the prosecution, the law enforcement agency that investigated the case, and others from the community who simply signed
up and asked to attend. On November 8, 2000, we all gathered at
the main state prison in Florence, Arizona, where the death house
is located.

In the early 1990s, Arizona changed from lethal gas to lethal
injection as the execution method. Just before three o'clock that
afternoon, the four groups were led separately though the main
yard of the prison, where all inmates were on lockdown. It makes it
very, very quiet. As the groups enter the small building containing
the execution chamber, there are risers for the attendees to stand
on. There is not much room. Burly prison guards stand between
the groups as if to keep us from attacking one another.

After we were sealed into the room, a curtain opened, and we
could see Miller on a gurney, a sheet up to his neck. He already had
the IV in his arm. Prisoners not only can see the people gathered to
witness their death but are allowed to make a statement to them.
Miller did, looking directly at Jennifer's brother, and apologized for
taking his sister's life. I'm not sure why he didn't address her parents,
but after saying what he did, the warden let us know that there
were no stays of execution entered and that they would proceed.

While there have been reports nationwide, including here in Arizona, of executions that did not go well, taking an extraordinary amount of time and possibly causing suffering, such was not the case with Don Miller. As we silently watched, the warden gave the signal to begin. Miller took a deep breath, exhaled, and was still. Within minutes the warden announced that the inmate was dead.

Eighteen years later, in 2018, Luna applied for parole for the first time, asking to be allowed to end his sentence for murder and begin his consecutive sentence for kidnapping. I appeared before the parole board and objected based on the senseless nature of the murder and Luna's new position that he'd been railroaded into taking the plea, that he'd had nothing to do with the murder. I reminded the board that Miller, the less culpable defendant, had been executed. Luna's request was denied, but he can apply again every year.

I had attended other executions both before and after Miller's. I can only say that I left each one asking myself what the point was. After years of litigation and enormous expense, it comes down to a small room and an anticlimactic end. There is no satisfaction, it is just finally over. Miller is dead and Luna is alive and could be paroled someday, as Judge Fleischman said, due to the vagaries of the criminal justice system.

VIRGINIA

One of the criticisms of the death penalty is that it is mainly the poor, less educated, and, in some states, minorities who are subjected to it. It is a valid criticism, as one need only look at the makeup of death rows across the country to confirm this. I don't subscribe to the opinion that prosecutors target that community for prosecution. Rather, there are a number of societal ills in this country that bring the poor and uneducated before the court, sometimes for very violent crimes. But as a prosecutor you also see cases that reject all the notions that the poor or persons of color have a monopoly on horrific murders. Such was the case with Dale Bertsch, MD.

In the late 1980s, Dr. Bertsch, a Phoenix anesthesiologist, and his wife, Virginia Depper, divorced after twenty years of marriage. Bertsch, as a high-wage earner, was ordered to pay Virginia spousal maintenance of three thousand dollars a month, which he paid for several years. The divorce was acrimonious, and Virginia was successful in persuading the divorce court that these payments were to be made through the court and then distributed to her. Bertsch was not to know where she was residing, not even in which state, nor allowed to send any funds directly to her. In 1993 Bertsch decided that he'd paid too much for too long and sought to change the status quo.

He reached out to the lawyers he'd used in the divorce and asked them to seek a modification of the divorce decree to reduce or remove the alimony requirement. At the time Bertsch was making up to three hundred thousand dollars a year and paying Virginia $36,000 spread out over twelve months. Bertsch threatened that if Virginia did not accept some modification that he'd disappear and she'd have nothing. Virginia replied that she'd see him in court. When Bertsch's lawyers told him there was no chance of any modification, he fired them. Then he demanded his case file, saying he'd find other lawyers who would do what he needed. He soon discovered he didn't need any other lawyers. His problem could be solved by his own hand.

In the file he obtained from his divorce lawyers was a small slip of paper with Virginia's address in Tucson. While there was some information that Bertsch thought she was living in Nebraska near family, for several years Virginia was living only a couple hours south of Bertsch on the outskirts of Tucson in a neighborhood where most houses were set on an acre or more. The doctor now had information that he'd lacked for years—and a plan to cut off all alimony payments forever.

On October 16, 1993, Bertsch rented a car in Phoenix, paying by credit card and using his own name. Twice over the next four days, residents in Virginia's neighborhood saw an older white man acting oddly around Virginia's house. Bertsch was sixty-three and white. They saw him with binoculars peering down the block toward her residence. One neighbor wrote down the license number of the rental car, another took note of Bertsch's odd behavior, and was later able to identify him from a photo lineup.

———•———

On October 20, 1993, Virginia was alone in the back bedroom of her house around 7:30 in the evening. She heard a noise coming from the darkness outside the window. When she looked out, she was immediately shot through the window, the bullet entering her chin and exiting the side of her face. Virginia ran from the bedroom to the dining room, where her phone was located. A blood trail led from her bed to where her body was later discovered.

Picking up the phone, Virginia called 9-1-1 and frantically told them that someone had shot her from outside her bedroom window and that she could hear them outside the house. They were breaking in. Virginia was bleeding profusely from her wound, and her voice on the 9-1-1 tape showed she was scared to death. She pleaded that someone hurry to her house.

The murder itself was captured on the emergency line audio tape. It was horrific, frightening, and heartbreaking. She began screaming and yelling at her attacker, so frightened that most of what was recorded was too difficult to discern. But one last gasp was clear, distinct, and ultimately the centerpiece of the state's case. With her dying screams, Virginia yelled, "No, Dale, don't!" As she fell silent, the tape picked up one sound, the repeated blows to Virginia's skull. One could almost hear the rage of her attacker with the sounds of the beating.

When sheriff's deputies arrived, Bertsch was gone. Virginia lay dead in her dining room, her skull fractured so badly that pieces of it were scattered around her. She had been shot once, then beaten to death in a rage by her former husband, a medical doctor. Given the neighbors observations of an older white man in a car acting suspiciously in Virginia's neighborhood and the astute neighbor writing down the plate number of the car, it didn't take long for detectives to figure out who had been there. They soon discovered the acrimonious divorce, Bertsch's attempt to modify the alimony or threaten to disappear, and an attempt by Bertsch to change paperwork at a Phoenix hospital that purported to show him in an operation at the time of the murder.

In August 1994, after a ten-day trial in which we played the 9-1-1 tape as many times as possible, the jury convicted Dr. Bertsch of first-degree murder. The state was going to seek the death penalty. The decision was not because the defendant was a well-to-do white, educated man but because the murder was horrifying. A medical doctor decided he simply didn't want to pay his ex-wife the money that she was due from their twenty-year marriage. He shot her through a window then beat down her door to attack her again. The savagery of the beating, in our minds, showed this crime to be one of the worst of the worst murders. Bertsch, we decided, should be subjected to the most stringent sentence allowed by law.

As this was the 1990s, the trial judge would be the one to decide the appropriate sentence. Bertsch was represented by a high-profile Phoenix law firm who had previously represented him in medical matters. The lead defense attorney, Larry Hammond, had decades of criminal experience, was smart, and knew his way around a courtroom and how to argue in front of a jury. While the facts were against him at trial, he and his team geared up for the sentencing hearing, which wouldn't take place for several more months. Bertsch, at age sixty-three, was facing either twenty-five years to life in prison or the death penalty. I felt, given the horrendous nature of the murder, he should be on death row.

The aggravating factors we alleged in the attempt to seek the death penalty were pretty straightforward. They were that Bertsch had committed the murder with the expectation of monetary gain and that the murder was committed in an especially cruel manner. The latter factor required that the state show the victim had consciously suffered during the murder. The 9-1-1 tape, we were convinced, proved that beyond doubt.

In April of the following year, the court began the sentencing hearing. Over several days the trial judge, Michael Brown, heard testimony from the state that included Virginia's family, the police detectives, and the case pathologist. The testimony from the family spoke about the relationship between Virginia and Bertsch during and after their marriage. The police and pathologist essentially covered the facts of the case again, reminding the court of the horrific nature of the murder, Virginia's suffering and the $36,000 in alimony that was the reason for the murder.

There were family members for the defense as well. Siblings of Bertsch came to court to talk about his good character and life history. Evidence of his medical training and work was brought forward, his lack of a criminal history argued, and the defense said that given his medical training Bertsch could somehow be an asset to the prison. It seemed a dubious argument that the Department of Corrections would allow a convicted murderer to work as a prison doctor, but anything is admissible as mitigation. Further, the attorneys argued that since Bertsch was an anesthesiologist, sentencing him to die by lethal injection amounted to cruel and unusual punishment in that Bertsch would be especially apprehensive about an inadequately trained executioner placing a needle in his arm. [As I stated, anything is admissible in mitigation.] The defense contended a life sentence, given the defendant's age and that he'd have to serve at least twenty-five years, was sufficient for the crime.

We felt strongly that if we were seeking the death penalty against younger offenders who had committed similar murders that Bertsch shouldn't get off with a lesser sentence just because of his age and his social and economic status. During the hearing, one of Bertsch's older brothers had testified about the family, his brother's upbringing, and his life as a doctor. He testified on a Wednesday. Two days later, on Friday, walking back into court, the brother suffered a massive heart attack and died before testimony was to begin that day. While that was very sad, we also felt it had little to do with the appropriate sentence for the crime the court had to consider. We were wrong.

On May 24, 1995, the court announced the sentence. I had to prove that Virginia had consciously suffered during the murder to meet the requirements of the aggravating factor of an especially cruel murder. And I had to prove that monetary gain was a motive for the murder. In my mind the evidence at trial and at the sentencing hearing clearly proved both of those factors. The judge announced that he found that neither of those elements had been proven.

As to whether the murder was for pecuniary gain, the judge ruled that the sum being paid in alimony simply didn't seem substantial enough to be the cause of the murder since Bertsch made so much more. That argument ignores the many murders we have over very small amounts of money. Instead the judge adopted something I had said to the jury in closing arguments at trial, that the murder showed hatred and all-consuming rage. As the court found this rage to be the primary motive for the murder, the judge ruled that I had failed to prove the murder was committed for monetary gain.

As to the second factor, in his verdict the judge stated that the evidence proved "beyond a shadow of a doubt" that Virginia's fear and anxiety were real, actually palpable, that she felt incredible terror in the last moments of her life. But, the judge ruled, the murder lasted less than three minutes, and while horrible and cruel, it was not "especially" so, that being the legal requirement. That was a judgement call by the court. He decided that the palpable terror that everyone could hear on that tape was cruel, but not especially so. Another judge may well have taken that same evidence and found that clearly the suffering was especially cruel. This judge had something else on his mind.

After finding that the state had failed to prove either aggravating factor that could lead to a death sentence, the judge excoriated me and my office for seeking the death penalty at all. He announced in court that given the defendant's age and the time it takes to appeal a death sentence that Bertsch would probably be dead before his sentence could be carried out. The court noted the cost of the death sentence as opposed to life in prison and called imposing a death sentence merely a Pyrrhic victory for the state.

I'd had issues with this judge both before and again after this case. His negative feelings about prosecutors in general were fairly well known, and my interactions with him were usually unpleasant. The fact is that the cost and the length of time to execution are, according to case law, legally irrelevant to the determination of the proper sentence. The court could have simply stated the state failed to prove the aggravating factors and left it at that and I could easily have accepted Brown's decision. Instead he had to rant about his opposition to the death penalty. He told those in the courtroom that in the face of a vigilante mob seeking the death of prisoners, our country had a history of judges upholding the Constitution and refusing to pander to the popular or succumb to vengeance.

I was infuriated with Brown. Not because of the sentence but with his grandstanding. I saw it as nothing more than playing for the TV cameras and trying to portray himself as the only one seeking justice. There was no vigilante mob, no outcry for Bertsch's death. Instead, Virginia's family had sat quietly and respectfully in court through trial and sentencing. There was no outcry from them or the community calling for a death sentence.

What I saw as disingenuousness in Brown's statements about the death penalty in this sentencing was demonstrated about five years later when I had another murder case in front of him in which he sentenced a seventeen-year-old kid to death.

———————

He ended his verdict with an observation about Bertsch's brother dying in court, stating, "There has been enough death in this case." Nothing the judge said was a legal cause about whether Bertsch deserved the death sentence. I don't think any other judge in the courthouse would have pontificated as much as Brown did and given the horrific facts, most would have imposed death.

But the randomness of the application of the sentence can come from prosecutors, juries, and certainly judges. Judge Fleischman had found Miller's crime to meet the legal standard of especially cruel, heinous, and depraved based on the facts of that case. Here, Judge Brown, faced with a murder certainly just as cruel and similarly committed for monetary gain, ruled that I had failed to meet the legal standard. Either case could have had a different outcome with a different judge.

In August 2018, Bertsch had a parole hearing, having served the first twenty-five years of his life sentence. He was eighty-seven and had virtually no disciplinary issues while in prison. I asked the parole board to listen to the 9-1-1 tape, and they did. After hearing it they agreed that Bertsch should stay in prison. He'll be eligible to apply for parole again in the summer of 2019.

THE PROSECUTOR'S DECISION

One of my favorite colleagues in the office to co-try cases with over the years is now the judge I mentioned earlier, Judge Godoy. But as prosecutors, she and I would get called out to most of the murder cases in our jurisdiction. We each had substantial experience in trying murder cases and significant experience in trying capital murders. We'd get called by law enforcement to murder scenes a lot. It gave us the advantage of seeing the evidence firsthand as the cops saw it. But oftentimes being at the scene also put into our minds whether the case merited being a capital one or not. Even before a suspect or a motive might be discovered, we were already thinking about whether we should seek the death penalty. It was based on our experience, the number of murders we'd seen, and our gut instinct. Once you have in your mind as a prosecutor that the case should get a death notice, it's hard to back away from that position.

One of the best examples of this manner of deciding to seek death was a case we did in the early 2000s. On November 28, 2000, the two of us were called out by the sheriff's office to a grisly discovery. In the desert northwest of Tucson, a hiker had discovered the body of a young woman. It turned out to be that of a nurse, Amanda, who had left her apartment the night before to return a video to the store. She'd never returned home. She'd been kidnapped at the store and driven miles across town to where her body was found.

Walking through the scene with the detectives, we took note of a number of things. The young victim had clearly been running away from her attackers. In the light of day, we could easily see Amanda's long strides through the desert floor showing that she'd tried to outrun the danger. She'd been shot in the back and fell facedown. Near Amanda's outstretched left hand was an inhaler she'd used for her asthma. A young woman, kidnapped near midnight and driven to a remote deserted location, had tried to flee her kidnappers by running through a cactus-strewn desert. The inhaler gave us a clear picture of someone that was likely scared to death and running for her life. Having such an innocent victim always would cause you to start thinking about the death penalty. But the scene revealed even more evidence that would shape our opinion early on about what penalty to seek.

After completing our walkthrough, and after Amanda's body had been removed by the medical examiner staff, the sheriff's department had decided to use the scene to test a new cadaver-seeking dog. The handler wanted to see if the new animal could find where Amanda had been laying. The dog wouldn't go toward the spot. Instead it kept pulling further away from where Amanda had been found. Several times the deputy would start over, but the dog kept pulling a different direction. Thinking there may be a dead animal somewhere near the crime scene, the handler let the dog pull him away. About one hundred feet from where Amanda had been found, the dog led deputies to another body.

———•+•———

We were called back. The body of a young man was laying under a tree not far from where Amanda was killed. Detectives found identification on him, and we soon learned that his name was Dana. He'd been reported missing nearly two weeks before and not seen since. Dana had been shot in the back of the head with a shotgun and left in the desert. Given the remoteness of the area, it was not a coincidence that the bodies were so close together. We had a person or persons that were killing multiple people after driving them to this uninhabited area. Before we'd left the scene the second time, my colleague and I had it firmly in our minds that whoever was responsible for this should be subjected to the death penalty.

In Arizona the only crime for which the death penalty applies is first-degree murder. But that crime can be committed in this state in various ways. First is the traditional or commonly under-stood premeditated murder, as in Agatha Christie novels where the suspect plans and carries out the murder with forethought. Most often our premeditated murders don't have that much planning. Someone decides to kill, and within a few minutes the murder is committed. These premeditated murders are the most common type of charge for first-degree murder and make up the bulk of potential death penalty cases.

There are two other ways in Arizona to commit first-degree murder. One is generically called felony murder, the other is the intentional or knowing killing of a police officer who was in the line of duty. Neither of these require premeditation, that is, no reflection of the murder need be proven by the state. Felony murder occurs when a death is brought about during the commis-sion of certain crimes. For example, if two men go into a conve-nience store to rob the cashier and during the robbery one of the robbers shoots and kills the clerk, both men can be charged with first-degree murder. Even if the nonshooter didn't know his accom-plice had a gun, the mere fact that he was participating in a robbery is sufficient to charge him with the murder. The death penalty can apply to this kind of offense; however, it is less common for the prosecutor to seek death in these cases.

For the murder of a police officer, no planning or premeditation is required for the prosecutor to prove first-degree murder. It is sufficient proof if the state proves the defendant intentionally or knowingly took the life of the police officer who was in the line of duty. I've prosecuted two cases of this type, and one defendant is on death row, the other doing life in prison. But even without proof of premeditation, the death penalty can apply in these cases as well.

As I mentioned in a previous case, the prosecutor is the sole decision maker as to whether a first-degree murder case becomes a capital one. While certain legal standards have to be met, it isn't at all difficult for the prosecution to meet them if he or she wants to seek the death penalty. In addition to the charge of first-degree murder, the prosecutor has to have proof of what's called an aggravating factor. Some states call them special circumstances. In Arizona, the existence of a single aggravating factor is enough for a case to be filed with a death penalty notice. Arizona has fourteen aggravating factors although a current bill before the State legislature may reduce that number. Knowledgeable prosecutors can usually find one of those fourteen in just about any case they have before them.

Most of the factors are designed to separate a "normal" first-degree murder from the truly awful ones. All murders are awful of course, but the law is that prosecutors are supposed to pick for the death penalty only the "worst of the worst." It's a pretty subjective decision as you can imagine. While prosecutors making these decisions have usually seen a lot of murder cases, picking the "worst" ones simply isn't very scientific. It's a gut feeling, but a decision made with experience behind it.

———

Some of the fourteen aggravating factors inherently separate some of the worst offenders. For example, someone who commits multiple murders at one time or a string of murders over a period of time meet some aggravating factors. A murderer who has been convicted of certain violent crimes in the past or kills for monetary gain would also meet the statute. Then there are some factors that are perplexing, even to prosecutors. The Arizona legislature has decided that a murder committed using a remote stun gun is an aggravating factor. This is something I've never seen in my thirty-five years as a prosecutor, but I suppose anything is possible. Another is whether the murder was committed in a "cold, calculated manner, without pretense of moral or legal justification." I can give a pretty good guess as to what that is supposed to mean, and I can allege it if I want to. But even with my experience, deciding that a case is without "pretense of moral or legal justification" is totally subjective.

While a court can review later, at the request of the defense, whether there is sufficient evidence to prove the factor or factors alleged by the prosecution, it's really a low bar to meet. I've yet to see a case where a judge felt he could strike the prosecution's notice of intent to seek the death penalty based on insufficient evidence of aggravating factors. The bottom line is that if the prosecution wants to seek death, there isn't much to stop the case from proceeding in that fashion. But how to make that decision is the question. It's got a long history.

From 2000 to 2002, I was a member of a rather large committee in Arizona called the Arizona Attorney General's Capital Case Commission. It was headed by then Arizona Attorney General Janet Napolitano before she became governor and later Secretary of Homeland Security. The commission itself was made up of thirty judges, legislators, prosecutors, defense attorneys, victim advocates, and others. The purpose of the commission was to study how the death penalty was being used in Arizona and whether it was just and fair. It seemed a fairly simple task and one that, given the makeup

of the commission and their experiences, would be somewhat intu-
itive to those already working in that system. It wasn't.

We learned quite a bit about the system that had existed since
the mid-1970s, when Arizona had brought back capital punishment after a brief nationwide hiatus. The US Supreme Court had
invalidated death penalty laws across the nation in 1972 as being
unfair to defendants in the manner the laws were being imple-
mented. Many states, Arizona included, had to rewrite their laws
to comply with the Supreme Court decision and allow for a fairer
procedure. The commission was formed to determine how we
had done. Arguably, the answer was that we hadn't done well at
all. Not because we found that innocent men had been executed,
but rather because the decision of prosecutors in seeking the
death penalty, and which murderers actually received it, was
pretty random.

After two years the commission made several recommendations regarding how the death penalty should be applied in
Arizona. But one recommendation had a big impact on my office
with respect to the number of cases where we sought death. They
drastically lowered over the few years after 2002. The commission
had studied five years of cases from around the state. We discovered
that no one, prosecutors included, had any idea of how often death
penalties were being sought or even who was making the decision
to seek death. That fact astounded me, and by then I'd had been a
prosecutor for twenty years. Here's what we learned.

In most counties in Arizona, individual prosecutors were
deciding whether to seek the death penalty in a particular murder
case they were assigned. No group met and discussed whether a
particular case met the legal standard to seek the penalty, and no
real guidelines existed to help the lone prosecutor make the decision
other than whether an aggravating factor existed. As a result, the

commission discovered that my county, Pima, was filing a death notice (the one-page document a prosecutor files to initiate a case as a capital one) in nearly 35 percent of first-degree murder cases. In Maricopa County, where Phoenix is located, the percentage was even higher. So much for the argument that the death penalty was reserved for the "worst of the worst." Instead it was pretty much a one-in-three chance the state would seek death if a defendant was convicted. Even more astounding was the discovery by the commission that when the state sought death, it was being imposed only about 17 percent of the time. Four out of five cases where a prosecutor filed a death notice resulted in a sentence of something other than the death penalty. The time, money, and resources spent in pursuit of the death penalty was mainly wasted.

My office changed our protocols in 2002 and instituted a rule that a panel of attorneys would meet, discuss potential death penalty cases, and decide whether the office should pursue the sentence. We would talk to victims, police officers, and defense attorneys, seeking their input and knowledge of the case, defendant, and crime. Partially as a result of this new panel, our filings of notices of intent to seek death dropped to around 6 percent of first-degree murder cases from the 35 percent it had been before. This was much more in line with what the US Supreme Court had envisioned by the worst of the worst. And, instead of 17 percent of those defendants actually receiving a sentence of death, the percentage climbed to almost 70 percent in my county. Fewer defendants were facing death, saving time, money, and resources, and a much higher percentage of capital defendants were seeing the sentence imposed.

But that wasn't the only change that came about in 2002. The US Supreme Court once again announced a decision that greatly impacted how death penalty cases could proceed. After the 1970's legislation was passed in Arizona to bring back the death penalty statutes that had been struck down, the state decided that judges, not juries, would make the decision as to penalty. Juries would hear the facts, decide whether the state had proven the case, and find the defendant guilty if the state had. Then a separate hearing would be held weeks after trial where only the judge would decide whether the defendant should serve life or be sentenced to death. This process had been upheld numerous times, including in a decision by the US Supreme Court in the 1990s. In 2002 however, the court decided they had been wrong. Only juries, not judges, could make the life-or-death decision the court decided in a case called *Ring v. Arizona.* Arizona once again had to change its laws.

There was much discussion about whether Arizona should retain the death penalty. Since the capital commission was shedding light on some of the problems we had, and as many members were the same legislators who would be voting on the new laws, there was speculation that Arizona might give up capital punishment altogether. It didn't happen. Instead, the laws were rewritten giving guidance as to how juries would now make the decision. Cottage industries became part of the Arizona capital case system, with mental health experts and other death penalty specialists from around the country ready to be brought in and testify in front of juries about the defendant.

As a jury had to make the decision regarding sentencing, the process of picking a jury became much longer. Jurors were informed they'd have to decide, if they convicted a defendant of first-degree murder, whether to impose a binding sentence of death. If a conviction is obtained, the penalty phase begins immediately with the same jurors who spend days, often weeks, listening to every detail of the defendant's life, background, history, and upbringing before making a decision. Trials went from lasting one to two weeks to two months or longer.

In the end, the percentage of defendants getting a death sentence went up because we were seeking fewer cases with murders that were truly awful but also because the facts of the cases were the worst things that these jurors had ever heard. There was no context for them. When judges made the decision, they could think of many other cases they'd seen and weigh whether the case before them was a worse murder than others. Jurors have no such experience on which to rely.

But with all the changes of the legal standards, as well as bringing about panels of experienced prosecutors to look at a case to decide whether a particular defendant should face the death penalty, the system allows for little objectivity. The decision remains one based on what the prosecutor's gut tells him or her. And there is little way around that. A prosecutor has to have at least one provable aggravating factor as discussed above. But if the decision to seek death is based just on the existence of an aggravating factor, then almost any first-degree murder would be eligible. The decision comes down to more than that.

When I'd get called to a scene like that of Amanda and Dana, it was always hard not to decide then that the death penalty should apply. While we would always wait for a panel decision, our opinions would, of course, be heavily considered by the group. Our impressions at the scene would stick with us, and a vote for or against seeking death would be largely based on those first impressions. It was hard to fight against it, and while not wrong, it was little different than when a single prosecutor made the decision.

The killers for Amanda and Dana were arrested and charged with both murders. The evidence showed the two men, Frankie

Rodriguez and John Harper, had randomly kidnapped both victims to rob them and steal their cars. We sought death against each in separate trials in 2002. The outcome of the cases sheds some light on how our initial decision can get changed.

Both men were convicted. Rodriguez was convicted of both murders. Harper was convicted only of the murder of Amanda. Harper's jury imposed the death penalty on him. Later though, a separate jury decided against death for Rodriguez, and a life sentence was imposed. That caused us to go back to court on Harper and withdraw the death sentence. We decided that with their involvement in the murders being equal, it was unfair for one to be on death row while the other was not. Even though perfectly legal, it was, in our opinion, not equitable. Both men are now serving life sentences without the possibility of parole.

The question then of how a murder case becomes a capital murder is not complex. The prosecution alone makes the decision, guided by the aggravating factors and any information provided by the defense, victims, or law enforcement. But it is instinct, based on experience, that brings about the final decision. One that is subject to little oversight until a jury hears the case, often years later.

DAVID BEAN PHOTOGRAPHY

GARY

Usually it is the prosecution's decision, a court's order, or a jury's verdict that results in a life-and-death decision. At times, however, it is some external factor over which the prosecutor, judge, or jury have no control. The United States is one of a few nations across the world still using capital punishment. It conflicts with the practices of most of our European and North American allies, and their opposition to the death penalty impacts the decisions that prosecutors make on some cases. That opposition can control the decision about whether to seek the death penalty, precluding the state from even considering the question. Such was the case with Pamela Phillips and the car bombing death of Gary Triano.

After several years of marriage, Pamela Phillips and Gary Triano divorced in 1993. Triano was a well-known and flamboyant Tucson personality. He had been a hugely successful investor in real estate and tribal gaming. Triano made, and lost, millions of dollars both for himself and investors, some from Mexico and China. At the time of his murder, he had large gambling debts in Las Vegas and had filed for bankruptcy reorganization, claiming $40 million in debts from investments.

Triano's business partners had described him as aggressive and demanding but also as someone who had a knack for making deals. At times in his professional life, he was worth millions. Such was the case when he married Pamela Phillips in 1986. Phillips, a former model and realtor, became a socialite in the Tucson scene upon marrying Triano. A photograph appeared of them in the local paper in 1990 when they attended a University of Arizona basketball game accompanied by another deal maker, Donald Trump, and his then-wife Marla Maples. Triano was living high. He had a multimillion-dollar home in a Tucson country club and a chauffeur, and he flew his own plane. There were plans for, and investors in, a casino project in China.

While life was financially good for much of the marriage, Phillips had claimed to a friend before the divorce that Triano had threatened her with a gun. Phillips told the friend that she could have Triano "taken out." She spoke of Triano's Friday golf habits and how easy it would be to find someone to kill him, stating that she had a life insurance policy on him. It would still be years before any of that would happen and almost two decades before that friend would come forward to police with this information.

Phillips filed for divorce and sought custody of the two young children she had with Triano. The court hearings were dramatic and acrimonious. Phillips filed for restraining orders against Triano, claiming he was prone to violence and carried a gun. She claimed he would show up at the house she'd kicked him out of, tear her clothes, and scare away the household help. On her end, Phillips would become infuriated with Triano, and in court once, she threw a cup of water on him. In the end, Phillips was awarded custody of the children, but Triano had visitation rights. After the divorce

Phillips moved with the children to Aspen, Colorado, although court battles regarding visitation with the children continued.

Despite the divorce and relocation to Aspen, Phillips maintained a $2-million life insurance policy on Gary's life.

In 1996 Triano complained to the court that Phillips was interfering with his ability to see his children and demanded intervention. Despite being divorced for nearly three years, their battles continued. In this instance, the court sided with Triano and ordered that unless Phillips provided the children for a visit with their father in Tucson over the Thanksgiving holiday, the court would find her in contempt and sanctions would be imposed. Gary didn't live to see the holiday.

While living in Aspen after the divorce, Phillips was trying to make a living in real estate. She was also trying to establish an Internet business, Star Babies, a service that prepared and sold astrological predictions of a child's life for new mothers. It was in this endeavor that Phillips met Ron Young. Young was a shady character who was eventually accused of defrauding a different business in Aspen. But he was just the person Phillips needed in her life at that moment.

While Phillips had some money from the sale of her home in Tucson before moving to Aspen, she was raising two children, trying to make a living, and facing high expenses in that mountain city. Now she had the added pressure of complying with the Tucson judge's order of sending the children to Tucson, at her expense, for the November holiday. After living a socialite lifestyle in Tucson, Phillips was living in a duplex in Aspen trying to keep her head above water.

Despite this, Phillips, with the help of Young, hired an au pair to look after her children. The au pair, Kevin, was actually a ski instructor who was looking for a cheap place to stay in Aspen during the ski season. He saw an ad that promised free room and board in exchange for a couple nights a week of watching the children. Kevin called the listed number, went for an interview with Young and Phillips, and was hired on the spot. Over the course of the ski season, Kevin's duties became much more involved than a couple nights a week of taking care of the children.

While Phillips spent many of her evenings at local country clubs, Kevin became the primary caregiver to the children. He got them up in the morning, fed them, and got them off to school. He taught skiing during the day and then made sure the kids were home and fed, and he helped with homework. He also became a confidant of Phillips, listening to her complaints about her lack of money and the need to acquire more. When not at the country clubs, Phillips was spending most of her time trying to get Star Babies off the ground. When she told Kevin she was almost out of money and didn't know what she was going to do, Kevin suggested getting a real job. Her reply was that she was going to meet someone at the club worth at least $20 million and get remarried.

In October 1996, a month before Phillips would have to comply with the court order and send the children to Tucson for Thanksgiving, Ron Young disappeared from Aspen. Phillips was still living in the duplex, still had Kevin working for her, was still working on getting Star Babies running, and was almost out of money. She was paying $500 a month to maintain the life insurance policy on Gary's life in the amount of $2 million. It was soon to pay off.

In mid-October, some residents in Brea, California, called the local police department about a van that had been left parked on the street in their neighborhood. It seemed abandoned and had Colorado license plates. An officer responded and, upon conducting a records check of the van, discovered it had been reported stolen by Avis in Aspen. Avis had rented it to a man named Ron Young, and he'd failed to return it, thus prompting the rental company to file a stolen vehicle report. While at the time police didn't realize it, later they found that Young's parents lived close by to where the van had been parked. He'd been visiting them.

The van was towed and inspected. The contents were perplexing. Inside officers found a shotgun, a map of Tucson, divorce documents for Triano and Phillips, and a list of names on paper. Seemingly random names, some with a type of car listed next to the name. Since the van was reported stolen out of Aspen, a detective from that police department traveled to Brea and took the car back to Aspen. He inventoried the items again, but none of it made any sense until two weeks later.

On November 1, Gary Triano was finishing up his weekly Friday afternoon golf game at La Paloma Country Club, a resort in the north side foothills of Tucson. It was a routine he stuck with each week, often with potential investors, taking advantage of the mild desert fall afternoons. It was an expensive habit, as the resort had high monthly fees, but one that Triano found helpful in recruiting new investors. Just after five thirty that afternoon, Triano walked to his car in the club parking lot, said good-bye to his companions, and got in. A few moments later, his car exploded.

The blast tore into Triano's skull, leaving exposed bone. Metal fragments of the bomb slammed into his head and torso. The explosion was so strong that the windshield and other parts of the car were blown as far as two hundred yards away. Although other golfers were finishing up, the only other person to be injured was a man in an adjacent car who was hit by flying glass. Triano died instantly.

News of the car bombing made the national news and papers. News of a golfer blown up in an upscale country club in broad daylight was something that made it quickly around the country, including Aspen. The next day, the detective with the Aspen police department who had catalogued the recovered van from Brea, California, read about the bombing murder of Gary Triano. He picked up his phone and called the sheriff's office in Tucson. Ron Young had some explaining to do. But Young had disappeared.

It took days for law enforcement to recover the evidence at the sight of the explosion. Pieces of Triano's car were spread out over the parking lot, the country club, and surrounding streets. Local, state, and federal law enforcement agencies were involved in the investigation. The Bureau of Alcohol, Tobacco and Firearms, ATF, brought in their bomb experts, who spent months sifting through the evidence, looking for bits and pieces that would tell them what kind of bomb was used and how it was constructed. It was a painstaking process. But through meticulous work, agents were able to reconstruct the device. It was a simple pipe bomb. Materials someone could buy at most any hardware store were used. A metal pipe with capped ends, filled with an estimated one pound of gunpowder and screwed to a wooden board, was used. A remote control that would power a model airplane, attached to a battery, allowed the bomber to be up to four hundred feet away and watch while Triano got into his car. The ATF investigators found the remains of a blue bag in which the bomb had been placed. It was simple and very deadly.

From the remains of the car, investigators were able to determine that the bag containing the bomb had been placed on the front passenger seat of Triano's car. His friends knew he never locked his car while he golfed, and he often left the windows down. This habit allowed someone to walk by the car, drop a bag on the front seat, walk away, and wait. From the autopsy showing the damage to his body, it became clear that Triano likely got into his car, saw the bag, and leaned over to open it. It was the last thing he did.

While detectives had an early lead in the news about Ron Young from Aspen, they determined there were a lot more suspects. Investors who'd lost money included wealthy individuals from abroad and within the States. Some investors were very connected, and not in a good way. Triano had also been involved in dozens of lawsuits. The sheriff, when pressed by reporters about leads as to who might be responsible, was quoted as saying, "Open the phone book."

While Ron Young was certainly among the people police wanted to interview, dozens of potential witnesses were contacted and interviewed. Colleagues, investors, and gaming people in Vegas and Atlantic City were contacted. Triano owed one witness with known mob ties $50,000. When detectives met with him in Florida, he granted an interview and admitted he was owed the money. But he said he wouldn't kill anyone over a mere fifty grand.

Pam Phillips was interviewed in Aspen multiple times by police. Her connection to Young and the fact that she had a large life insurance policy on her ex-husband certainly seemed suspicious to police. But her explanation about the insurance was that in the event of Triano's death, she needed to provide for the children. As to Young, she noted that even before the murder she had filed a police report in Aspen against him, claiming, as had some other businesses there, that Young had defrauded her.

While Phillips was a concern and the van recovered in California perplexing, the investigation continued for years. First, dozens of detectives from a variety of agencies were involved, but eventually the team whittled in size. The leads were not getting anywhere, and by the early 2000s, there had not been much progress in finding the killer. Ron Young had vanished off the face of the earth. Meanwhile, in January 1997, Phillips collected on the life insurance policy of $2 million and moved from her duplex into an Aspen showcase home.

In 2005 detectives decided on a new approach. Unable to find Young through extensive normal police work, detectives sought help. Warrants for Young's arrest had been issued in Aspen for the reports of fraud dating back before the bombing. Detectives approached the television show *America's Most Wanted* and asked if they'd be willing to profile Ron Young and the attempt to find him for fraud. The bombing wasn't to be mentioned. The show agreed.

In November of that year, the show aired, showing pictures of Young and his connection to Aspen and allegations of fraud. The information was now going nationwide to see if any viewers might have information about Young's location. It paid off. The morning after the show aired, a chiropractor in Ft. Lauderdale called the number provided by the series. The man pictured was a patient, although he was known to the doctor by a different name. He was scheduled for an appointment that very day. Officers in Broward County, Florida, were notified, and by that afternoon Ron Young was in custody. A lead that had long eluded the sheriff in Tucson was about to break the case wide open.

Detectives from Tucson flew to Ft. Lauderdale the next day and began speaking with Young. Meanwhile, a search was conducted on his apartment and storage shed and on his laptop computer. The material they found astounded the detectives: boxes of computer storage drives, hundreds of recorded phone calls, and thousands of emails and accounting spreadsheets, all detailing contacts between Young and Pam Phillips, stretching back years, back to the time of Gary Triano's murder.

So much information was seized that it would take months for detectives to sift through it, listening to phone calls, reading the emails, and having FBI forensic accountants review the many spreadsheets that detailed payments made from Phillips to Young in small amounts lasting from 1996 into the early 2000s. While they failed to discover a "smoking gun" about Triano's murder, the picture developed by the detectives clearly showed a debt owed by Phillips to Young that she was sending to him in cash each month through a parcel service. The emails and recorded phone calls between the two convinced investigators they had found Gary's killers.

While investigators continued to review the evidence, Young was sentenced to prison time on weapons charges stemming from his possession of a gun while being a fugitive. Him being in custody allowed for time to figure out what had happened between Young and Phillips and how it led to Gary's murder. Phillips in the meantime had moved to Europe, where her daughter was attending school. In 2008, twelve years after Triano was blown up in his car, a grand jury in Tucson indicted both Pam Phillips and Ron Young for the murder. Young had been released from prison by then and was selling sandwiches in California. Detectives served an arrest warrant on him, and he was brought back to Tucson to stand trial. A similar warrant was issued for Phillips, but the complexities of extraditing someone from Europe would delay her arrival back in Tucson for two years.

Ron Young went to trial in early 2010 and was convicted of first-degree murder and conspiracy to commit murder. Three months after that, Pam Phillips was brought back to Tucson to face the same charges. In July of that year, a judge ordered she be held on a $5-million bond. It would still be nearly four years before she would face a jury. In 2013, while preparing for Phillips's trial, the two prosecutors in the office who had been working on the case for years and had conducted the Young trial both left the office. The county attorney asked that I and a colleague get ready to try Pam Phillips. There were dozens of banker's boxes of evidence, three hundred thousand documents, and scores of witnesses. My co-counsel, Nicol Green, thought it sounded fun. Fortunately, Phillips's defense team wasn't ready for trial, and the judge ended up giving us a year to prepare. In early 2014, we began a trial that lasted eight weeks.

The evidence we had, gathered over the course of the previous eighteen years by law enforcement, was laid out before the jury. While the jury picked for Phillips's trial was not legally allowed to know that Young had already been convicted, the defense team asked the judge to inform the jury of that fact. They intended to show not only that Phillips was innocent but that Young was wrongly convicted. The jury was going to hear a lot about Young anyway. The information gathered by detectives about Phillips's finances, the life insurance, and her relationship with Young was presented to the jurors. But it was the treasure trove of material that Young had saved and police recovered in Florida in 2005 that was most damning. The jury was presented with an account out of *Lifestyles of the Rich and Famous*. They heard about millions of dollars earned and lost, elegant homes, and a nasty divorce. Then the jury got to hear the recorded phone calls, see the emails, and examine the accounting spreadsheets. Together they told an unmistakable story of greed and violence.

The FBI forensic accountant explained to the jury that the discovered spreadsheets were amortization schedules that showed payments in cash from Phillips to Young in the amount of $400,000. It was paid over several years, usually in payments of less than $2000 at a time, and always in cash. FedEx records proved that Phillips was sending a package to Young, under an assumed name, once or twice a month to Florida. The payments were established through these accounting sheets, but it was the emails and phone calls that revealed what they were for.

The two would exhaustively discuss the money in hours of

phone calls recorded by Young. At times they would discuss the police investigation into Triano's death. Phillips would send emails with FedEx routing numbers and when to expect the payments. This payment method began in 1997 and continued for years until the relationship began to wear on them both. After years of such payments, Phillips began requesting an accounting of how much she had paid and how much she still owed. Young sent her the amortization schedule, and Phillips then learned that Young was charging interest of the money owed. Phillips was livid. Young explained that she was earning interest on "his money" and that it was owed to him. She had gotten her 1.6 Young reminded her, and he got his 4.

When Phillips threatened to stop sending money, Young told her that she was living on money that she had because he had helped her with a problem that no one else in the world would have helped her with and she was benefitting from it. When Phillips balked at sending any more money, Young replied that he had information that would send her to a woman's prison for murder.

The jury had heard enough. After eight weeks of trial and nearly one hundred witnesses, the jury deliberated two and a half days. Phillips was convicted of the same charges as Young, first-degree murder and conspiracy.

The murder of Gary Triano had been committed for pecuniary gain, the $2 million in life insurance. That monetary gain motive is an aggravating factor that can often lead prosecutors to file a notice of intent to seek the death penalty if there is a conviction. In addition, Gary's death was arguably cruel and depraved, another aggravating factor used to assess the filing of a death notice. Here though, our hands were tied. Phillips could never face the death penalty.

Because she was found in Austria and we were at the mercy of governing officials in the European Union, those officials set conditions for the return of Phillips to Arizona. Working with US State Department officials, my office had to agree in writing that we would never seek the death penalty for Gary's murder. If we failed to agree, the officials in Europe responsible for her custody would simply refuse to extradite. We had no choice but to agree.

While some murderers escape the ultimate punishment because of decisions of prosecutors, jurors, or court decisions, Phillips could not face death because of the opposition European governments have to capital punishment, a factor outside the control of prosecutors but no less arbitrary. On May 22, 2014, at age fifty-seven, Pam Phillips was sentenced to the rest of her natural life in prison. She will never be eligible for parole.

INTERNATIONAL RESPONSES

As I explained in the last chapter, I could not seek the death penalty on Pam Phillips because in order to have a successful extradition from Austria, my office had to officially declare in writing that she would not be exposed to a possible sentence of death. We committed that we would not file a notice to seek death. Such a filing would be the only way a jury could consider that sentence, and our agreement precluded a jury from sentencing her to death.

Some questioned why the state couldn't file a notice and seek the death penalty once she was returned and in our custody. There are several answers to that. First, we had given our word to the extraditing authorities in Europe that we would not do so. Ethically and morally we would not go back on our word. Practically speaking, for future requests of extradition of other murder suspects, our word would be worthless if we disregarded our commitment, and other nations could refuse to turn over suspects. Failing to abide by our agreement would undoubtedly have consequences for future cases. We could also be sued, as was the case in 1999 through 2001 at the International Court of Justice (ICJ) in The Hague.

In 1982, half-brothers Karl and Walter LaGrand committed a bank robbery and murder that my office prosecuted. The brothers had gone to a small bank in Marana, a town in the greater Tucson metropolitan area, and waited for bank employees to arrive. Once the manager arrived, the brothers showed him a gun, which later proved to be a toy but nevertheless gained them access to the bank.

Shortly thereafter one of the tellers arrived, and both employees were held hostage by the LaGrand inside the bank.

When the manager stated he only had half the combination to the safe and couldn't open it, the manager and teller were tied to chairs and repeatedly stabbed. The manager suffered twenty-four stab wounds and died. The teller suffered multiple stab wounds but survived to testify against the brothers. Another employee had arrived at the bank while all this was happening and had had the composure to write down the license number of the car that Karl and Walter had driven to the bank.

Law enforcement quickly found the two, and in 1984 Karl and Walter were tried by a jury and convicted of the murder and robbery. Because of the nature of the murder of the manager and attempted murder of the teller, the office had filed a notice that we would seek the death penalty. At sentencing, still in the days in Arizona where only the judge decided the penalty, both men were sentenced to death.

Karl and Walter had been born in Germany of a German mother and were therefore German citizens. Both had moved to the United States when they were four and five years old and had been adopted. Although both remained German citizens, they grew up in this country and spoke and acted like US citizens. Neither told investigators at the time of their arrest that they had foreign citizenship.

———

In 1963, the United States had signed a treaty called the Vienna Convention on Consular Relations. Part of that document called for signatories to notify other member nations when one of their citizens had been arrested. The intent was that a country might provide for legal services for their citizen or at least send a representative to speak with them. Obviously that didn't happen with Karl and Walter, as investigators were unaware at the time and neither brother brought it up. Later the state conceded that by 1984 the issue of citizenship had arisen but no one, not the prosecution, the defense, or the court thought to notify the German consulate of the case.

Some ten years after being sentenced to death, the brothers heard about the Vienna Convention and notified the German government that they were on death row in Arizona. German authorities began to seek relief from the Arizona governor's office and other US officials. Only when appeals had been exhausted on the criminal conviction and a date set for execution did motions begin to be filed.

After their appeals had failed, the Arizona Supreme Court ordered an execution date for Karl for February 24, 1999, and Walter on March 3, 1999. The German government sought relief from the US Supreme Court, the president, the Arizona governor, and the Arizona Board of Executive Clemency based on the argument that the United States had failed to abide by its commitment to the Vienna Convention. The first three declined to intervene, but the clemency board recommended the governor stay the executions for sixty days. That request was refused. On February 24, Karl was executed at the Arizona state prison.

On March 2, 1999, German authorities filed a request with the International Court of Justice in The Hague, Netherlands, arguing that the violation of the treaty obligations were sufficient for the ICJ to issue an order that Walter's execution be stopped. On March 3, the court did just that. The order stated that:

> *The United States of America should take all measures at its disposal to ensure that Walter LaGrand is not executed pending the final decision in these proceedings, and should inform the Court of all the measures which it has taken in implementation of this Order.*

Later that night, Walter was executed in Arizona despite the order.

The suit against Arizona continued for two more years with the ICJ hearing arguments about the failure to abide by the treaty obligations and what remedy was appropriate. In June 2001 the ICJ issued a final judgment finding that the United States had breached its obligations under the Vienna Convention, depriving Germany of the possibility to render assistance to its citizens. The court also found that the United States breached its obligations to the court by failing to stop Walter's execution after the March 3, 1999 order.

In the end, Germany rejected the idea of any monetary compensation, and the court found that future cases, if any, should be subject to review and reconsideration of any conviction and sentence. While there were really no sanctions of significance, prosecutors have an obligation to follow the law. Other nations take those obligations seriously. Take the case of my office's prosecution of a Canadian citizen for the murder of his wife.

In October 2006, Henry Fischbacher, a Canadian citizen, was living here in Tucson with Lisa, his wife of twenty-three years. During an argument on the evening of October 5, Fischbacher beat Lisa severely with a flashlight and then dragged her outside to the pool where he held her head underwater for several minutes. He then left her body at the pool, caught a flight to Buffalo, New York, where he rented a car, and drove into Canada to the home of a relative. The next day Fischbacher's sister contacted law enforcement to tell them her brother had called her and confessed to the murder of his wife. When deputies arrived at the house, they found the victim floating in the pool, blood inside the home.

Within a few days I had drafted a complaint charging Fischbacher with first-degree murder and requested State Department help with an extradition from Canada to stand trial. It would take three years for Canada to release him for transport to Arizona to face charges.

To support our request, the Canadian authorities required a great deal of information from us. Not just the charging documents needed to be supplied but Arizona statutes on the charges and any sentencing provisions that applied. In addition, we had to provide all the law enforcement reports about the investigation for their review. It seemed as though each time we provided the requested documents, the Canadian government had additional requests for information.

As I mentioned previously, we take such dealings with foreign governments very seriously and would never think of reneging on any agreement we entered. We were already prepared for the expected request that the death penalty be taken off the table in the case and thought, given his confession to his own sister, Fischbacher would be back in Tucson fairly quickly. But the Canadian court system had other ideas.

Fischbacher's Canadian lawyers filed a challenge to our first-degree murder charge, arguing that the circumstances of the murder, under Arizona law, amounted to no more than second-degree murder, that is, an intentional killing without premeditation. It was the first time I'd seen a foreign court get involved in what a defendant might be guilty of rather than just ordering that extradition hinged on our willingness to forgo a death sentence.

The argument was made initially to the minister of justice of Canada, who refused to make the distinction between first- and second-degree murder based simply on the police reports. The Canadian Court of Appeals had no such hesitation. Comparing Arizona law to Canadian law regarding different types of murder, the court found that based on the sudden argument described by Fischbacher that his crime was only that of second-degree murder, they ordered that the minister reconsider his decision to extradite the defendant based on the conclusions the court had reached about the varying degrees of Arizona murder statutes.

———•———

In November of 2009, just over three years after the murder, the minister of justice made his final decision. If we agreed not to seek the death penalty, we could have the defendant on the charge we had initially made, first-degree. We agreed, and later that month Fischbacher was in the county jail. Within a few months, he pled guilty to second-degree murder and was sentenced to prison.

While we are usually successful in getting a suspect returned from a foreign country, assuming they are located there, it doesn't always work out that way. Our request to the Chinese government to extradite an accused murderer ended up quite differently than what we had expected.

In the fall of 2001, a Chinese student was attending the University of Arizona and living near campus with his wife, also a Chinese national. Jianquing Yang and his wife, Yuyun Chen, lived in a quiet neighborhood with their six-year-old daughter. Jianquing was a doctoral student in chemistry at the university. On the morning of November 4, 2001, a 9-1-1 call was received by police from the six-year-old. She stated that she could not wake her father and thought he might be dead. Her parents had always told her that in the event of an emergency she should call 9-1-1. When police arrived they found Jianquing and Yuyun had been stabbed repeatedly, he lying on the stairs of the two-story apartment, she lying dead in the living room. Both had died of multiple stab wounds, and blood surrounded both deceased.

Oftentimes in such murders, the attacker accidentally cuts himself in the frenzy of the stabbing. It isn't uncommon for the murderer to leave his own blood behind at the scene, which helps police in the investigation. Such was the case here. While both victims had bled profusely from the multiple wounds, police found other drops of blood in the kitchen, some distance from both Jianquing and Yuyun. Given the scene, police suspected the attacker had cut himself and attempted to clean his wound in the kitchen.

In speaking with friends and family members of the victims, police discovered that the two had recently befriended another Chinese national named Wenshi Zhou. Yuyun had met Zhou at a local restaurant where she had worked part time. Jianquing and Yuyun were members of a Tucson Baptist church and over the course of the several weeks before the murders had spoken to Zhou about their religion. The pastor of the church described Zhou as having "no peace in his heart." According to friends, just before the murders, the couple had for some reason severed ties with Zhou.

Based on this evidence, investigators went to the apartment Zhou shared with two other relatives. Zhou was gone, they said, having been driven by them to the airport early that very morning after he claimed to have gotten an emergency call that his wife was ill in China. He got on an early flight to Los Angeles and thereafter to Beijing, paying cash for a one-way ticket. At the time police were still investigating the scene, Zhou was on his way to China, where he in fact did have a wife and child.

The police lab was able to quickly analyze the blood drops from the kitchen found by detectives and compare them to DNA samples taken in Zhou's apartment from items belonging to him and from samples of DNA taken from his relatives at the apartment as well. The blood left in the kitchen of Jianquing and Yuyun's apartment belonged to Zhou.

Like we do in most cases, the facts were presented to a grand jury, who issued charges of first-degree murder. We obtained a warrant and filed our usual extradition papers through the State Department, seeking assistance in getting the suspect back to

Tucson. While the European Union and Canada do not have the death penalty, China uses the sentence frequently. We didn't expect to have to agree not to seek death but rather have the man handed back over to us. Given the two murders committed in a heinous manner, we would potentially file a notice of intent to seek the death penalty once he was in our custody.

By the middle of December, Chinese police in Guang Dong Province had found and arrested Zhou. But rather than the Chinese government allowing extradition back to Arizona, my boss, who was the elected county attorney, and I began to get visits from Chinese consular officials and police investigators. As with other countries we had dealt with, the Chinese officials wanted all of the police and lab reports and all the witness statements taken by detectives. We had two visits, each time given gifts from our visitors. The second visit included a Chinese security official from the embassy in Washington, DC, who spoke impeccable English and had an impressive background in international criminal investigations.

He explained that police in China had interrogated the suspect and spoken to the victims' family who lived in the same city where our suspect was captured. The six-year-old daughter had been taken back to the area by relatives as well. It was the desire of the relatives to see justice done in China where they lived. The Chinese investigators had read our reports, labs, and witness statements and decided to deny our extradition request. The murder case, they said, would be tried in China. The security official explained to us that under Chinese law, since both the defendant and victims were Chinese citizens, jurisdiction lay with them. The official very politely, but just as firmly, told us that his government would "handle the matter." While we weren't entirely sure what he meant by that, we had no recourse. Although our visitors had said they would tell us the outcome of the trial, our efforts to contact anyone in the Chinese government weeks, then months, later went unanswered. We could only assume that a trial was held and some sort of justice was carried out.

Over the years, I've spoken to citizen groups and classes at various schools about the death penalty. A slight majority of Americans, polls show, still support capital punishment. I've met citizens of other nations where the death penalty has been abolished and gotten their reactions to the United States still having the sentence. Of course they vary, but most of my interactions have ended with the other person saying that their country had evolved and found it unfortunate, some say barbaric, that we still employ the practice.

In 2014, my youngest daughter, Laura, now a lawyer herself, received a Fullbright to teach English language skills and American culture to secondary students in the small town of Kapfenberg, Austria. While one might think that had little to do with capital punishment, over the course of teaching every day for a year, she tried to offer the students a variety of subjects. Someone suggested a class on the US justice system. Laura solicited my help. I had a presentation I'd given many times on capital punishment that contained some of the cases discussed here and many others. The facts of each case were outlined with gruesome detail.

Since I cautioned that the subject might be too much for high school students, Laura previewed the PowerPoint with her supervising teacher, and the school decided it would be a good lesson. Any student could opt out, but the remaining students would see some awful murder cases discussed. She said the students found it to be one of the more fascinating lectures she gave. Each of her classes throughout one day, both semesters she was there teaching, got the lesson. The teachers in the school requested their own presentation.

Austria, being part of the European Union, does not have capital punishment, but the topic kept their attention. They were shocked at the gruesome nature of the murders. However, even with the horrible details of what some people can do to another, most of the students and teachers simply said that the death penalty was wrong. They were equally shocked that Laura, a young woman just out of her undergraduate work at the time, knew so much about murder. She told them how she grew up with it being part of the dinner table conversation as the daughter of a prosecutor.

In August 2018, Pope Francis declared the death penalty to be wrong in all circumstances. While the Catholic Church had been leaning that way for some time, it was the first time that a pope had clearly and unequivocally stated that capital punishment was wrong and should not be used under any circumstances. The impact of the Pope's declaration may take some time to assess. Within two days of the announcement, at least one Catholic governor and other politicians stated the declaration would not change the way they conducted criminal justice. Internationally, most majority-Catholic nations already ban the death penalty throughout Europe and South America. But such an announcement may certainly have an impact on the way people in this country view the punishment. That "slight majority" in the polls could be falling.

MELISSA, JAMES, BOB

At about two o'clock on the morning of January 18, 1999, my phone rang. The Tucson Police Department homicide sergeant told me that about three hours before, late on the seventeenth, officers were called to a Pizza Hut on the east side of town. The manager, Robert Curry; the seventeen-year-old busboy, James Bloxham; and the twenty-one-year-old waitress, Melissa Moniz, had been shot to death in an apparent robbery. I was requested to come to the scene to render legal advice should it be needed.

The restaurant was several miles away, but at that time of night, it didn't take long to get there. When I arrived, the parking lot of the convenience store next door was full of police cars flashing red and blue lights. The main road in front of the restaurant had the same. As there was a blood trail in the restaurant's parking lot, it had been sealed off, as well as the restaurant itself, to preserve evidence inside. But my attention was focused primarily on a small group of people standing near the police command post, a large RV that served as a communications center and working space for the detectives. The people standing outside were the family members of the victims who hadn't come home when the restaurant closed, and were silently waiting to find out what had happened.

The detectives had me put hospital-like booties over my shoes and led me into the restaurant. They explained that the blood trail in the parking lot was from Melissa, one of the victims, being transported by ambulance to a hospital. Police had found her still alive inside, but I was informed she had died shortly after arriving at a local emergency trauma center. Jimmy and Bob both lay dead inside.

While prosecutors are normally called to a crime scene to help with legal advice for such things as search or arrest warrants, the additional advantage to later prosecuting the case is the ability to see things firsthand right after they happen. While hundreds of pictures are taken by police photographers and reports written by each officer in attendance, being able to view the crime scene and picturing what happened is invaluable in later arguing the case to the jury. I'd been to literally dozens and dozens of such scenes.

Bob and Jimmy lay on their backs behind the counter and register. Each had been shot multiple times, the exact nature and number of shots would be determined at autopsy. That examination on the three victims would reveal that Melissa had been shot in the head, neck, right arm, and hand. Jimmy had been shot in the head, chest, abdomen, and left leg. Bob died of gunshot wounds to the head, neck, and chest, that bullet ripping through his name tag. The robbers had been unable to open the register or the safe and left with the bank bag, which contained only checks from the shift's diners. Bob had separated the cash already, and it was left behind. Later the detectives discovered the checks had been burned, meaning that the three victims had been not only sense-lessly murdered but the robbers got nothing.

At one booth in the restaurant still sat the plates, knives, forks, and napkins of the people that had occupied the table. Detectives found bullets, bullet fragments, and shell casings throughout the restaurant. Everything was photographed and collected and would be submitted for DNA analysis. It was a grisly scene as I was escorted around and eventually back outside. The family members still waited and watched in silence as detectives authenticated the identities of the victims and attempted to make some sense of the inside. Then, with the help of victim advocates, the families were informed of what they clearly had already feared.

News of a triple murder gets out on television and radio quickly, reporters coming to these crime scenes in an effort to report live about any details police can share. Before the next day was over, detectives received a phone call from a young man named Josh who had information about the murders. Josh reported that sometime after midnight into the early morning hours of January 18, seventeen-year-old Christopher Huerstel and nineteen-year-old Kajornsak (Tom) Prasertphong, came to his house and asked to sleep there until morning. It was there, according to Josh, that Huerstel described how he and Tom had decided to rob the Pizza Hut with Prasertphong's gun. Huerstel described to Josh how he shot Melissa in the neck and then "continued to the back."

Josh gave the police information regarding the location of the two, and later that day detectives arrested both men standing outside of Prasertphong's truck, which they had driven to the restaurant the night before. The men were separated, searched, and taken to the police station to determine if they would answer questions. The truck was seized and taken to the station to be searched.

Prasertphong, a native of Thailand who'd been living in the United States for many years, told the police that while he spoke English, he sometimes didn't understand "bigger" words. After being read his rights, he agreed to give a statement. He told police that he and Huerstel had gone to the restaurant and that, while eating, discussed robbing it. He claimed that he was unaware that

Huerstel had carried Tom's .40-caliber Glock handgun into the restaurant. Prasertphong stated he decided not to do the robbery, as there was a woman, Melissa, and that he'd given her his debit card to pay for the meal.

Huerstel, according to Tom, had gone into the bathroom and come out shooting. He first hit Melissa and then began demanding that Bob open the safe. Tom told the detectives that Huerstel then shot Bob and then Jimmy, who was behind the counter. Prasertphong saw that Melissa was still breathing, and he grabbed her by the hair, looked at her, and tried to snap her neck. When that didn't work, Huerstel shot Melissa in the head. They grabbed the bank bag of checks, and Tom grabbed the debit machine, apparently thinking that would destroy evidence of his card being used. He admitted that when they found the bag contained only checks that they burned the contents and threw the debit machine in a wash. They hid the handgun in the wheel well of the spare tire of the truck and went to play pool before ending up at Josh's house later.

Based on Prasertphong's admissions, the detectives found the bank bag, debit machine, and the murder weapon still concealed in the wheel well. They then went to the room where Huerstel had been placed and was waiting.

The detectives had actually spoken to Huerstel once, and he had denied any knowledge of the murders and denied being at the Pizza Hut. Going back into the interview room, the detectives played a portion of Prasertphong's statement about the killings. Huerstel then admitted being involved and agreed that he had shot all three victims but added that Prasertphong had taken the last shot at Melissa, killing her.

The detectives continued their investigation, locating friends of Huerstel who admitted he had told them of plans to commit a robbery. The DNA tests on the plates and forks in the booth inside the store showed both defendants present. Ballistics tests on the Glock showed it to be the murder weapon. The case was two young men killing multiple innocent people in a robbery that gained them nothing. The office decided to seek the death penalty against both men.

In Pima County, murder cases get assigned to a judge by the presiding, or chief judge. The presiding judge in 1999 was the same judge who I'd had disagreements with in the Bertsch case described earlier. When a case is assigned, either the defense or prosecution can, within ten days of assignment, request another judge be assigned and no reason is required. The presiding judge assigned the case to himself. As soon as I saw the order come out, I filed my motion to have a different judge assigned, which typically is honored with no questions asked. This time it was different. Despite having filed my motion the day the assignment was released, I'd noticed the date of the order was eleven days prior. Thinking it must have been a typo, I ignored the date and filed my motion. I'd been waiting and looking each day for the assignment, as I had no desire to be back in front of this judge. The presiding judge is also the one who rules on the requests for reassignment. He denied mine, saying it was untimely by one day. When I protested that the order had only been issued, the judge shut me down, pointing to the date. While I'll never know if he deliberately withheld publication of the order until it was too late to file a request, I was now stuck in front of him again. It would be difficult.

Prasertphong was appointed the local public defender's office, who assigned three very experienced and good lawyers to his case. Huerstel was assigned a private lawyer who contracted with the court. In addition, Huerstel's family hired another private lawyer with over forty years of criminal defense experience. I considered both of Huerstel's lawyers friends, but that means little when the stakes are as high as they were in this case.

There is a basic principle of law that when two defendants in a single case each confess but implicate the other in the crime, they have to have separate trials. The idea is that a jury should decide the guilt or innocence of a defendant based on the defendant's own statement, not what the other defendant has said happened. As such I didn't object to the inevitable motion for separate trials filed by both defendants. It should have been a quick, easy decision for the court.

Rather than grant the unopposed motion to sever the trials, the judge decided on a different path. While ordering that the trials would be legally separate, the court decided to try the cases at the same time in the same courtroom, but with each defendant having a separate jury who would hear only the evidence admissible against the defendant whose case they were to decide. This dual jury idea, while rare, was something I'd done before, but this was different.

———————

Typically in a dual jury trial, virtually all the evidence would be admissible against both defendants except for the presentation of their individual statements. Both juries would be present in court for most of the trial, only leaving when the prosecution presented the confession of the other defendant. Then they would trade places with the other jury, going out while the other defendant's statement was presented. It can work smoothly. In this case, all the attorneys argued against a dual jury trial. The evidence and witnesses were going to be very different against each of the men. There was no way, we all argued to the court, that we would avoid having one jury or the other constantly in and out of the courtroom so they wouldn't be tainted by evidence that was not admissible against both defendants. The arguments fell on deaf ears.

Not only was the court determined to try the cases together, the judge decided that because of pretrial publicity the case had to be moved out of the county and tried elsewhere. After telling us he'd researched courtrooms around the state, the judge announced he had found the only courtroom in Arizona that could accommodate two juries. We were, the court said, to try the case in Prescott, some two hundred miles from Tucson. That meant that the lawyers, court staff, defendants, and most important, all the witnesses would have to be transported over two hundred miles, given places to stay, and per diem for food. It was a logistical nightmare. For the several weeks of trial, witnesses were transported up and housed and fed at Prescott hotels. The attorneys were driving home on Fridays after court and returning on Sunday nights so they could spend time with their families. Only the judge managed to spend the entire time in Prescott, a charming town in the northern part of the state.

From mid-August until late September 2000, the two juries took turns going in and out of the courtroom so they wouldn't be exposed to testimony that was inadmissible against the defendant whose case they were tasked to decide. It was constant. Not only that, the judge's announcement that the courtroom would hold two juries proved untrue. While there was one normal jury box, the second jury was assigned to folding chairs near the gallery. The acoustics would challenge us every day, experimenting with microphones, moving jurors, and simply speaking loudly. There were hundreds of exhibits for trial, some admissible against both defendants, some exhibits only admissible against one of them. The clerk, whose job it was to swear in witnesses and keep written track of the daily rulings, also had to track the exhibits and make sure one jury didn't see an item they weren't supposed to. It was, as I said, a nightmare.

The case against Prasertphong finished a full week before that of Huerstel. We sent the Huerstel jury home for a day so we could do closing arguments in Prasertphong's case. After arguments and while that jury deliberated down the hall, Huerstel's jury came back to hear another week of testimony. After a day of deliberations, Prasertphong's jury had reached verdicts, but because reporters were all over the courthouse watching, the verdict had to be sealed without announcing the jury's decision. The jurors were sent home and instructed not to tell anyone what happened for fear that Huerstel's jury would hear and be impacted by the decision. The dual jury decision was proving to be a problem.

Things got worse after we did closing arguments the next week in Huerstel's case. The jury deliberated for three days before eventually announcing that one juror refused to discuss the case anymore after some heated arguments in the jury room. As we had with the issue of dual juries, the defense attorneys and I found ourselves in agreement once again against the court's proposed solution to the apparent impasse. The judge brought us into chambers after the note about the one juror. In the office was a man unknown to either the defense attorneys or me. The judge introduced the man as a social worker who he intended to send into the jury room to consult with the juror who refused to talk. One doesn't have to be a lawyer to know not only how improper this would be but also totally unconstitutional. It would be an automatic violation of the defendant's right to a fair and impartial jury.

In the meantime the court sent in a series of instructions to the jury concerning their deliberative process. Shortly thereafter, Huerstel's jury announced they had reached verdicts as well. Both juries were scheduled to be brought back the next day to announce their decisions: guilty on all counts for the murders of Melissa, James, and Bob. Since this was before jury sentencing became required in 2002, the same judge who had excoriated me for seeking the death penalty against a medical doctor some years before would now decide the sentence for a seventeen-year-old as well as the nineteen-year-old.

Sentencing for both men was put off until March 2001. First, because jury sentencing in capital cases was becoming a major topic nationwide, we litigated whether a jury had to decide the sentence for the defendants. The US Supreme Court had been inconsistent about this issue. While holding that it was constitutional for judges to decide the sentence, the court had recently issued an opinion that seemed to back off that stance but was still a year away from deciding that a jury had to decide the sentence. Our judge, after much litigation and argument, ruled that he alone would make the decision.

In Arizona the law states that the court *shall* impose a sentence of death if the court finds one or more aggravating factors and that there are no mitigating factors sufficiently substantial to call for leniency. While there was plenty of aggravation in this case, there was also mitigation the court could find and, in its discretion, decline to impose the death penalty. It was a decision totally at the discretion of the court. Sentencing day came for both on March 16, 2001.

The court had no choice but to find the aggravating factors I had alleged. The killing of more than one person was the main statutory factor. In addition, the fact that the murder was committed for monetary gain had also been proven. As to reasons for leniency, strong arguments could be made. Huerstel was only seventeen at the time of the murders, with no significant criminal history. Prasertphong, nineteen, had no criminal history either. Over fifteen hundred letters poured in from around the world from Amnesty International, the Thai consulate, and many others writing in an effort to persuade the judge not to impose death.

The same judge who a few years before had lectured me in court about seeking the death penalty for a sixty-three year old doctor who had shot and beaten his ex-wife to death was now poised to make the decision again. He could easily have declared that the age of the defendants alone was sufficient in his mind to show leniency. Instead, he repeated comments made by Justice Harry Blackmun years before, stating, "I am pleased that this case represents the last time I will have a hand in starting the state's machinery of death." He then imposed the death sentence on both of them. The judge had already made known his intention to retire from the bench.

Once a death sentence is imposed, an appeal to the state supreme court is automatic as I've mentioned before. The process often takes years to complete. Within a year, however, we knew the cases were coming back, at least for another sentencing. In 2002, the US Supreme Court, in a death penalty case out of Phoenix, finally decided that it was unconstitutional for a judge alone to make a sentencing decision imposing the death penalty. Only juries could make that decision. By early 2005, the court had also declared it unconstitutional to impose a death sentence on someone who was under the age of eighteen at the time the crime was committed. Both Huerstel and Prasertphong had to come back to court.

Because he was seventeen at the time of the murders, Huerstel could not get the death penalty. But the Arizona Supreme Court also weighed in on his case regarding the trial judge's actions during the Prescott trial. Finding that the judge had coerced the jury's verdict with his series of notes to them, Huerstel was granted an entirely new trial, one where he could not face the death penalty. Prasertphong's case was sent back to face a sentencing trial, this time in front of a jury.

Because we felt it inequitable that Huerstel could not get death and he was equally responsible for the murders, we ended up withdrawing the death penalty in Prasertphong's case. Since legally we were barred from seeking the penalty against one defendant, we decided not to seek it against the other. Due to issues with his attorneys and Prasertphong not getting along and awaiting additional rulings from the Supreme Court, it wasn't until the end of 2006 that Prasertphong was finally sentenced once again. Because we weren't seeking death, a judge imposed the sentence. Prasertphong would spend the rest of his life in prison.

Huerstel's case became more complicated, with issues of witnesses and evidence being litigated for some additional years. Ultimately, he entered pleas of guilty to lesser crimes of second-degree murder in early 2007. After years of litigation and lengthy trials, the imposition of death sentences, and decisions by the US Supreme Court that wiped all that away, Huerstel will be released from prison when he is forty-two years old, having served twenty-five years for his participation in the murders of Melissa, James, and Bob.

Sometimes I wonder what lesson is to be learned from this case. The murders of three innocent restaurant workers by two men looking for a small amount of money is horrific. Because the Supreme Court decided to change the rules shortly after their trial, both men escaped the ultimate punishment. We spent nearly a decade litigating every aspect of the case only to end up where we probably could have with a settlement and plea in the first year of the case. The anguish caused to the victims' families, the expense of multiple lawyers, and the cost of trial could have been avoided.

———•——

What I can say is that if the death penalty was not an option, the trials of the two defendants would have gone much differently. I've no doubt that their convictions in the trials would have been upheld on appeal. The two would have been sentenced to life in prison and the victims' families would have been able to move on from having the court proceedings dominate their lives. Instead, the possibility of the death penalty prolonged the agony of the crime for the victims, cost years of litigation, and ultimately, because the Supreme Court decided to change the rules right after our trials, we settled the matter with both defendants in prison for lengthy terms.

While seeking the death penalty initially in this case wasn't necessarily an arbitrary decision (after all, three innocent people were gunned down) the criminal justice system itself made it arbitrary by constantly changing the rules by which we operate. Had Huerstel been a few months older at the time of the murders, he could still have faced death. The Supreme Court set the age at eighteen. There are numerous studies about the adolescent brain not being completely formed until sometime into their twenties. The fact that Prasertphong at nineteen could still face death while Huerstel at almost eighteen could not doesn't make much sense from a scientific or psychological standpoint. But the law likes a clear demarcation line, so eighteen it is for legal purposes. The court could just have easily said twenty-one or twenty-five. From time to time I think about the trial judge's comments that he was glad it was the last time he was involved in the "state's machinery of death." While he and I disagreed on a lot of issues, something else he said while making this statement rings true. We are "beset by a plethora of convoluted statutes, conflicting and inconsistent court decisions, and constitutional interpretations." In short, the system is arbitrary and unworkable.

LAURA

On September 18, 1980, Laura Webster, a student at the University of Arizona, went with a friend to the Green Dolphin, a campus area bar. Laura never returned home. After being at the bar a short time, Laura was approached by Scott Clabourne and Larry Langston, who, after talking to her for twenty minutes, convinced her to go with them to what was described as a party. Had Laura known that the two men were parolees at a local federal halfway house, she likely would never have left the bar with them.

As they departed in a car accompanied by a third man, Langston, the driver, pulled over and grabbed Laura out of the car. He beat her then threw her back into the car and drove to a house Langston had frequented. Laura pleaded with Clabourne to help her and protect her from Langston, to no avail.

Once at the house, the men forced Laura to remove her clothes and serve them drinks. Langston continued to beat her, and all three of the men raped her. For six hours Laura was made to serve drinks to the men while they took turns raping her vaginally and anally and forcing her to perform oral sex on them. At the end of the evening, Langston told Clabourne to kill Laura.

Clabourne wrapped a bandanna around Laura's neck and strangled her. Langston handed him a knife, and Clabourne later admitted that he stabbed her twice in the chest, killing her. Laura had suffered hours of beatings and rapes and the horror of not knowing what would happen to her. The men wrapped her body in a sheet and drove to a bridge over a dry river bed, where they threw her into the wash below.

The next day, Laura's body was found and examined by the police and pathologists. The autopsy revealed the sexual assaults and sodomy, and it appeared from the examination that the stabbing had occurred after Laura had been wrapped in the sheet. The pathologist discovered Laura had not died from the strangulation but had still been alive when wrapped in the sheet and then stabbed.

At the time, police had no suspects and no leads. No one at the Green Dolphin could identify the men Laura had left with, and the investigation languished. It wasn't until a year later that a girlfriend of Clabourne's approached detectives to tell them that he had confessed to killing a young woman a year before. Police found Clabourne in the county jail on other charges and questioned him. After being given his Miranda warnings, Clabourne confessed to Laura's murder and gave details of taking her from the bar and beating and raping her. He implicated Langston, stating that he killed Laura only because he was afraid of Langston and thought Langston would kill him unless he carried out the order to kill Laura.

———————

Through Clabourne's confession, detectives were able to find Langston and the third man. Langston, a career criminal, did not talk. The third man confirmed Clabourne's story but denied any involvement in Laura's death, stating only that he was present. He was later convicted of hindering prosecution.

Given the facts of Laura's murder, the state decided to seek death against Clabourne and Langston. While Clabourne had given a full confession to the rape and murder, the evidence against Langston was much weaker, consisting mainly of Clabourne's statement, which would be inadmissible at a trial against Langston, the third man's statement, and a jail house snitch who also implicated Langston. Complicating the case against Clabourne was his history of mental illness and whether he was competent to stand trial. The fact that somehow the police had lost the samples taken during autopsy showing Laura had been sexually assaulted complicated matters further.

Several months after Clabourne had been questioned and arrested, he was evaluated by two psychiatrists, and while there was a documented history of mental illness, both doctors found Clabourne to be competent to stand trial in that he understood the proceedings against him and was able to assist in his defense. Thus there was no legal bar to trying him before a jury.

In late 1982, two years after Laura's body was found, in a five-day trial, Clabourne was convicted of her death and sexual assault. The evidence against him was mainly his own taped confession and the testimony of his girlfriend to whom he had first admitted the murder. Because it was still twenty years before the Supreme Court would require jury sentencing, Clabourne's fate was in the hands of the trial judge.

In January 1983, with little comment, the trial judge sentenced Clabourne to death, finding the statutory factor that Laura's murder had been committed in a cruel, heinous, or depraved manner had been proven and that there was no mitigation sufficient to call for leniency. A dozen years later, an appellate court determined that

Clabourne's lawyer had done an ineffective job at the 1983 sentencing hearing and ordered that the hearing be conducted once more.

In August 1997, a different judge heard the case for sentencing. The facts had not changed, and the murder was still one of the more gruesome and senseless killings that most judges would see in their time on the bench. The new attorneys for Clabourne presented much more extensive information about his life, detailing his previous mental illness and medication. The lawyers brought up new information that had not existed at the time of the original sentencing, that Langston had been offered and entered a plea after Clabourne's trial that allowed him to escape the death penalty. Thus, they argued, a death sentence for Clabourne would be unfairly disproportionate. The lawyers also convinced the judge to find that economic costs of the death penalty over life imprisonment was a factor to consider in mitigation.

This time the judge made much more specific findings. While acknowledging the mitigation presented, the court found that Laura's physical and mental suffering from being beaten and raped for six hours was especially cruel. The fact that Laura begged Clabourne for help further demonstrated her conscious suffering. The evidence from the autopsy that, after being strangled, Laura was still alive when Clabourne stabbed her with Langston's knife convinced the judge of her physical suffering as well. The judge decided these facts outweighed any call for leniency. On August 8, 1997, Scott Clabourne was once again sentenced to death. As of today, over twenty years after his resentencing, Clabourne is still on death row appealing his sentence. Larry Langston's case took a much different path.

While the other cases in this book were ones I either tried in the guilt phase or on retrial, my involvement with Langston came about in a different way. In late 1983, the prosecutors handling the case against both men had to decide whether to try Langston to a jury or seek some other disposition. The case against Langston was weaker than the one against Clabourne. After all, Clabourne had confessed, and there was evidence to corroborate that confession. Langston had not made any admissions, the police had lost the autopsy samples, and the state had a jail house snitch who, while giving the police details about the murder that he said came from Langston, had mental issues of his own.

There was another big difference between the two men that had to have given the prosecutors pause about dealing with Langston. While Clabourne had a minimal criminal history (the detectives had found him in jail on some property crimes after his girlfriend had told police of the murder), Langston was not only a career criminal but a violent one at that. In the twenty years before Laura's murder in 1980, Langston had been in and out of prisons across the country. He'd been given lengthy sentences for robbery, robbery by assault, and bank robbery but had always obtained early parole. The night he and Clabourne murdered Laura, Langston had been placed on parole from a Georgia bank robbery and was supposed to be at a halfway house in Tucson.

The prosecutors didn't want to risk a jury trial with the evidence they had against Langston. In December 1983, three years after Laura's murder, Langston entered a plea to first-degree murder and was given the only available sentence at the time other than death. The court sentenced him to life in prison with the possibility of parole after serving twenty-five years dating from the day of his arrest. Langston would be parole eligible once again in his lengthy criminal career while Clabourne sat on death row.

While I was in the office as a prosecutor during the pendency of these cases, I was new and not involved in the handling of the defendants. That would change in 2006, twenty-five years after Langston's arrest. In May of that year, Langston became eligible for release. Clabourne was still then, and now, fighting on appeal.

———•———

I began reviewing the case of Laura's murder and Langston's past history. While I certainly can't fault the decision in 1983 to plead Langston, as the case was not as strong as that against Clabourne, it was also clear that Langston was the driving force behind Laura's death. (Further, I had done the same thing in the case of Don Miller and the murder of Jennifer Geuder in pleading Joe Luna.) But the law would allow Langston a chance at parole after serving the twenty-five years. I decided I had to go to the parole hearing and let them know who Langston really was.

In preparation I not only reviewed the file and the appellate rulings, I met with the lead detective, who had long been retired, and also with Laura's parents, who by 2006 were approaching eighty years of age. The thought of one of Laura's killers being released was devastating to them, and the idea of having a hearing at which the details of the murder would be brought out again was extremely painful for the parents. But they were prepared to go through it.

Parole hearings are unique events. Anyone can speak to the board either on behalf of the inmate or the victim. There really are no rules other than showing respect to the witnesses and to the board members. The Arizona Board of Executive Clemency, as it's called today, is made up of five members appointed by the governor. Collectively they have sole authority to parole an inmate or keep him in prison on the life sentence. Their parole authority and decisions control the fate of any inmate sentenced for a crime occurring before 1994. Crimes after that were subject to a change in the law that gave more guidance regarding an inmate's release.

In May 2006, I appeared before the board members for the first time on Larry Langston, although I'd been before them on other inmates a number of times. Langston's case caused me to think back about Miller and Luna and the comments made by Judge Fleischman about the "vagaries of the criminal justice system." Here was yet another example. The person most responsible for a murder gets more lenient treatment. While legal, it is inherently unfair.

I stood before the board at the first hearing along with Laura's parents. They could barely speak about Laura's death and the impact it had on their lives, still painful after more than twenty-five years. They spoke of her smile, her laughter, and her intelligence, all taken away by Langston in 1980. For my part, I told the board members of the facts of the case and read from the Arizona Supreme Court opinion that had upheld the conviction and sentence of Scott Clabourne. That court, after reviewing the entire case, found that Langston was a manipulative and frightening man who had choreographed the crime. The court stated the evidence showed that while Clabourne inflicted the stab wounds, it was at Langston's direction. They called him a "frightening sociopath" who was the mastermind and influenced, even scared, Clabourne into committing the crime. And while Langston had escaped the death penalty with his plea agreement, it was not a legal bar to Clabourne receiving it. The mastermind of Laura's murder was eligible for release.

What is inherently unfair, yet totally legal in our death penalty jurisprudence, is that those most responsible for a horrific murder at times escape the ultimate sentence because of factors that have little to do with their culpability for the crime itself. As with Langston and Miller, the strength of the evidence, or some weakness to the case, allow the more culpable to get a lesser sentence while those against whom the evidence is stronger face execution. The "vagaries of the criminal justice system" seem a poor excuse for the disparate treatment that is seen time and again.

As for Langston, the board voted unanimously to deny parole in 2006. Under Arizona law an inmate sentenced at the time Langston was can apply for parole every six months after serving the first twenty-five years. For twelve years, except for one waiver of a hearing, Langston had a hearing every six months. Each time, Laura's parents would listen in by phone after appearing in person the first time and hear the facts of Laura's murder being recounted. At each hearing I would appear and read to new board members how Langston was a "frightening sociopath" who should never be released. I described his life of criminal conduct and how after each time he was released from a sentence he committed an even more violent offense. For his part, Langston would tell the board he was older, ill, and just wanted to live his life. Each time his release would be denied. It was a dance I suspected would continue for many years.

In the middle of June 2018, I was informed by the Department of Corrections that Langston had died in prison. After spending more than thirty-five years in custody, that part of the case was finally over.

Clabourne, thirty-five years after being sentenced, remains on death row while his appeal is still being fought on his behalf. Given Langston's repeated efforts at release, I suspect Clabourne will be the first person to wonder about the arbitrary application of a death sentence.

RHIA

On June 18, 2009, seven-year-old Rhia Almeida left her family home and rode her bicycle two blocks to the house of a young friend and classmate to see if he could play. Rhia and her family lived in a quiet neighborhood in the small town of Ajo, some two hours west of Tucson. It was a short ride that Rhia had made many times. Rhia's mother, Elaine, had never before had reason to worry about her daughter's safety in their quiet town. Elaine would never see Rhia alive again.

When Rhia knocked on the door of her friend's house, it was answered by the friend's older brother, nineteen-year-old Kyle Alegria. He was the only one at the house, the rest of the family was away for the day. Alegria brought Rhia inside and closed the door. Inside the home, Alegria brutally beat, sexually assaulted, and stabbed the young girl before taking her body to a nearby wash and leaving her under some trees.

When Rhia failed to arrive home after what was to be a short play time, Elaine sent her sons to bring her home. The young boys knocked on the Alegria front door only to be told by Alegria that Rhia was not there. Rhia's brothers saw her bike parked outside the home and ran back to tell their mother what had happened, sparking a search for the young girl.

Shortly thereafter, Alegria's family arrived home from their day's outing to find him washing bedsheets and cleaning the house with bleach. When Rhia couldn't be found, Elaine called both her husband and the sheriff's office while she continued searching the neighborhood. It was only a short time before deputies found Rhia's body in the wash where she had been placed by Alegria.

The pathologist who conducted the autopsy on Rhia's body would later tell the jury that there were massive head injuries with multiple blows to Rhia's forehead and back of her head. Alegria had inflicted numerous stab wounds to Rhia's face, neck, and chest. One chest wound was so forceful that the knife nearly penetrated through the skin on Rhia's back. In addition, there were injuries to Rhia's vaginal area, causing bruising to her cervix and leaving external bruising as well. In short, Alegria's assault was vicious and prolonged. Rhia had undoubtedly suffered during her murder.

After finding her body, deputies began questioning neighbors to determine if anyone had seen anything. Detectives went to Alegria's house and interviewed the family, discovering that everyone but Kyle had been gone for the day. Alegria's father told the detectives about the bleach and bedsheets. One neighbor told detectives that he'd seen Alegria walking toward a vacant house a short distance down the street carrying a bag. When detectives searched that house, they found that Alegria had hidden bloody clothes and towels there. While Alegria had tried to clean the room where he'd killed Rhia, forensic testing showed Rhia's blood on the floor. The clothing and towels he had attempted to hide had traces of Rhia's blood on them. There was no doubt about his guilt.

Alegria was arrested and indicted on charges of first-degree murder, kidnapping, and sexual conduct with a minor. Two colleagues in my office were assigned the case and reviewed the evidence against Alegria. Three months after his arrest, my office filed a notice of intent to seek the death penalty due to Rhia's age and the manner of her death. As with all victims' families, Rhia's was consulted on the case. As anyone can imagine, the emotional pain was almost too much for them to bear. But they had doubts about the death penalty. Although Rhia's mother had no experience with court cases and especially capital murder ones, like many victims she did not like the idea of the state seeking the death penalty in the name of her child. And she knew she was looking at years of litigation. The decision however rested with the prosecution.

It would be more than four years before a trial was held. From the time of the 2009 arrest until early 2012, Alegria's mental competency to stand trial was litigated. The law requires that for the state to try someone, that person needs to understand the nature of the proceedings against him and be able to participate meaningfully with his attorneys. Alegria had previous diagnoses of mental health issues and had once been committed as a juvenile to an in-patient mental health facility. The judge on the murder case needed to make sure Alegria was legally competent to stand trial.

At least four psychologists and a psychiatrist evaluated Alegria's mental state to determine if he was fit to go to trial. In early 2012, the court held multiple hearings to hear testimony. Ultimately the judge ruled that Alegria was not competent and committed him to a program at the county jail that would attempt to restore him to competence. The process of restoring competence involves in-patient treatment by psychologists and other mental health professionals working daily with a patient on both his mental needs and making sure he learns and understands the legal system. The Pima

County jail program is well respected. While it normally might be a three- to four-month process, it was well into 2013 before the doctors believed Alegria was ready for trial.

By that time my colleague who had started the case had left the office and asked me to take over the case for trial. I met with Rhia's mother and stepfather in Ajo and listened to their concerns and questions. They had been anxious for Alegria to plead guilty and get a prison sentence and have the case come to an end. Alegria, however, wanted his day in court. In February 2013, the judge determined that he was competent and could assist his attorneys, and he set trial for late that year. Alegria's attorneys filed a notice that they intended to present a defense of insanity at trial.

Given the fact that Alegria had previously been diagnosed with mental problems and Rhia's mother wishing for a resolution of the case, I talked to the defense attorneys about a possible plea. While normally once we file a death notice we don't negotiate about a plea, the circumstances here seemed to call for a settlement. The defense attorneys, however, stated Alegria wasn't interested. They said he saw the trial as a way to commit suicide.

———

In declaring a defense of insanity, the defendant admits that he committed the crime charged but alleges that he did so only because of an existing mental illness that prevented him from knowing his acts were wrong. While numerous psychologists had evaluated Alegria after his arrest, the defense hired a psychiatrist from San Francisco who had testified in many cases around the country regarding alleged insanity. He and I did not get along. I found him condescending and arrogant. He seemed to feel the same about me. I interviewed him before trial, and he told me he had not read any of the police reports in the case. I found this odd, as the doctor would have to explain to the jury why he thought given the defendant's actions of hiding clothing and attempting to clean the blood from the house after the murder fit into his theory that Alegria didn't know what he'd done was wrong.

The psychiatrist's report claimed that Alegria suffered from a long-standing mental illness, and in the doctor's opinion, Alegria committed the murder not knowing his conduct was wrong. The report, in several places, stated that Alegria would "riff" about various topics. I took that to mean he would go off on unrelated tangents when speaking with the doctor and thought the use of the term "riff" was simply a term the doctor used to explain that. At trial, the doctor attempted to tell the jury that hiding bloody clothing, using bleach to clean the blood from the house, and hiding Rhia's body all fit in to his opinion that Alegria didn't know his conduct was wrong. It was clearly a stretch.

On cross-exam, I asked the expert about not reading the police reports, something that all experts should do in these cases. He told me he had been in error and that he really had. But he never tried to correct that error. My cross went on for a while, taking him through all the defendant's actions the day of the murder that showed he clearly knew the wrongfulness of his conduct. The doctor was displeased with me. When I asked about the defendant "riffing" with him, the doctor paused, looked sternly at me, and then accused me of insulting him, his family, his city, and his religion. I hadn't done any of that, but such was his disdain for me. The jury could tell we didn't get along.

In such a case, the state also gets to hire a doctor and have an independent evaluation. I hired a neuropsychologist living in Tucson, Dr. James Sullivan, who had also testified in numerous cases, sometimes for the defense and sometimes on behalf of the state. I had used him in other cases and got along with him well.

What I liked most about Sullivan was his ability to explain his eval-uation in plain terms and not get caught up in a lot of terms no one would understand. He did well in front of juries.

The defense of insanity allows my expert to conduct his own testing and clinical evaluation of the defendant. Since the defense is that the defendant committed the crime but didn't understand it was wrong, the state's expert gets to discuss the events of the crime asking a defendant why they did certain things, such as hide the bloody clothing and attempt to clean the house of blood. The answers all go toward the ultimate opinion as to whether, despite any potential mental illness, the defendant knew his actions were wrong.

———•———

Sullivan spent hours with Alegria, talking to him about the crime and attempting to get him to take a battery of psychological tests to measure intelligence, personality, and whether there was evidence of malingering, that is, faking of symptoms. Alegria was willing to talk but refused most testing. Sullivan called me after-wards to tell me that not only did he believe Alegria was not insane at the time he had killed Rhia but that Alegria had told Sullivan that he knew what he was doing, knew it was wrong, and killed her anyway. No one, Sullivan told me, had fully confessed to him before.

Trial started October 8, 2013, and lasted into November. The potential jurors were told that if they were selected for the case, they would be deciding not only guilt or innocence, but that if they found Alegria guilty, they would also decide whether he would live or die. Many people going through the selection process simply cannot bring themselves to sit on such a jury. Others simply don't think they can sit and listen to evidence about the rape and murder of a child. To be tasked with making such a decision is more than many wish to take on. I can't blame them. Jurors are told that if they find the defendant guilty and choose death, it is not an advisory verdict but that the defendant will be sentenced to die. It takes a while to select a group of citizens who will take on that responsibility.

Prosecutors have differing opinions about what kind of people they try to select for a jury. While it is typically a cross section of the community, I like to get some people on who are well educated and have strong opinions about current events. They make for interesting jurors. We had that for Alegria's jury, and the foreperson was a retired lawyer who practiced civil law for the Department of Justice. It was a smart jury.

For a month the jury listened to evidence. First about Rhia and her horrible death. They had to view pictures of the crime scene, Rhia's body, and the hidden clothing. They heard from experts on insanity and Alegria's history of mental health issues. The guilt phase of the trial ended with the jury rejecting the defense of insanity and the testimony from the California doctor. They found Alegria guilty of murder, kidnapping, and sexual assault of Rhia. But they were far from done. They still had another two weeks of testimony to decide his fate.

As I mentioned previously, the defense is entitled to present all manner of evidence in an effort to persuade the jury to reject death and impose a life sentence. For several days the defense called witnesses who testified about Alegria's family background, his upbringing, and his education. Evidence was presented about his previous in-patient treatment for depression, and his girlfriend gave evidence about his odd mannerisms when they were together. Instead of the San Francisco doctor, the defense had hired a psychologist from Boston and another from Texas. The latter explained to the jury that, in his opinion, given Alegria's family background and previous mental health issues, it was all but predictable that he would be involved in a serious offense. The crime, he said, as I had heard him say in many others cases, was the product of a broken foundation early in life that was never fixed.

The Texas psychologist was part of this cottage industry of experts who travel the country testifying in capital cases. He had long before closed his practice and made a considerable living telling jurors about the broken foundations of childhood that led to predictable criminal behavior later in life. He had testified in several cases I had prosecuted with the same message in each. In Alegria's case he was on the stand a full day showing the jury slides and giving his opinion that the defendant was essentially doomed from the beginning of his life. He is paid between $20,000 and $30,000 dollars for each case to render his opinions.

———•─•——

One of the most emotional parts of the sentencing phase of the trial is the time when the victim's family is allowed to give an impact statement. The law requires the court to allow a representative of the victim, in this case Rhia's mother, to make a statement to the jury about how the murder has affected the family. The victim's survivor is allowed to tell the jury about the victim, what she was like, and what their loss has meant. It is a time like no other in court.

The prosecutor has to make sure any statement meets the requirements of the law. The US Supreme Court has set limits on what can be said to a jury by a victim's family member. The Arizona Supreme Court has further defined what is appropriate. The impact statement by a victim cannot advocate for either a death sentence or urge a life sentence. The statement cannot address the defendant directly but must be given to the jury and tell them what the murder has done to the family and how they have coped.

While I have seen some statements by victim survivors be PowerPoint presentations set to music with rotating family pictures, such a presentation has always struck me as impersonal. I explain to the mothers and fathers and others that, while they get to choose how to present their statement, simply sitting and telling the jury about their child, showing a photograph of her, and saying how much pain remains is the most effective way of getting their feelings across.

Elaine sat with me at counsel table and did just that. She brought a framed photograph of a smiling, beautiful Rhia, and for a few minutes told the jury how much she missed her only daughter. She told them of how she saw Rhia ride her bike down the street that day and how she could never fully recover from what happened after. It was impossible for anyone to hold back tears. It was a simple statement of a mother who missed her daughter and whose life would never be the same.

What Elaine was not allowed to tell the jury, despite me knowing full well her position, was that she and her family hoped the jury would not impose the death penalty but rather give a life sentence. She did not want to relive the events of the murder over and over each time there was an appeal. She did not want to wait decades for the case to be closed. She did not want the state to execute Rhia's murderer in her name. She wanted Alegria to go to prison and never come back and to not have to be repeatedly reminded of how Rhia was killed. But a short time later, I stood before the jury and asked them to sentence Alegria to death.

I mentioned earlier the types of jurors I like on a panel: educated, involved, and mindful of what they are asked to decide. My belief is that despite the seemingly mindless restrictions of the law that don't allow the mother of a murdered child to tell the jury what is best for her family, this jury saw the pain they would inflict on Elaine if they were to impose death. The jury chose life.

My thoughts were proven correct later when the court excused the jury. Sometimes jurors like talking to the attorneys on either side after an emotional case just to let some feelings out. I ran into about three-quarters of the jury outside the courthouse after they were let go. They stopped and talked for a long time. The foreperson, the retired civil lawyer, knew a bit about capital punishment, although he had never practiced criminal law. He told me the jury talked about the horrible facts of the crime and how badly they felt for Elaine and her family. In the end they decided they could not put Elaine through years more of suffering by not bringing the case to a close now. The jury knew that a death sentence would bring years of appeals, even though that fact was never discussed by the judge or the attorneys. They knew because they were educated and informed about events in their community. The jury decided to put an end to the litigation.

I was fine with the jury's decision. I felt I had done my job the best I knew how, presented the evidence, and argued as passionately as the law allowed me to do. I was somewhat conflicted about asking for death given Elaine's feelings, but I was following the law that the people of Arizona have decided they want. My job was to use my best judgement, apply the law as fairly as I knew how, and seek what was the appropriate punishment. But part of me couldn't help but be relieved for Elaine and her family that they would be spared decades of appeals and future hearings.

The expense of putting on a capital trial, even just through the trial phase is high. The experts charge enormous fees for their preparation and testimony. The judge had asked the foreperson about the defense expert from Texas who testified for hours, as we had all seen the foreperson taking a tremendous number of notes. To our surprise, the answer was that in order to stay awake during this long, often boring, testimony, he had decided to make grocery lists, to-do lists, anything that would keep him from nodding off. The decision of the jury to impose life had to do with their feelings about what a death sentence would do to Rhia's family and little to do with anything the lawyers or experts had said.

On December 9, 2013, four and a half years after Rhia's murder, the judge sentenced Alegria to the rest of his natural life in prison. In early 2017, after his one appeal, Alegria's conviction and sentence were affirmed. His case is closed, and he will never be eligible for release. He will die in prison. Another jury might have imposed death based on the horrific facts of this case. But on that day, it wasn't a judge, a prosecutor, or an appellate court that made the decision. This jury decided that day that life in prison was sufficient.

11

JANUARY 8, 2011

Shortly after ten o'clock Saturday morning on January 8, 2011, in Tucson, time stopped for our community. A mass shooting that killed six and injured thirteen others brought the world's attention to this city and knocked the collective breath out of those who live here. A young man with previous mental health problems had been able to purchase a Glock handgun with an extended magazine holding thirty rounds of ammunition. In his mental illness, he had focused rage on one of our congresswomen, Gabrielle Giffords. That morning, while Gabby held a "Congress on Your Corner" meeting outside a northwest Tucson grocery store, Jared Loughner ran up to Giffords, who was talking to constituents along with members of her staff.

Loughner began firing at Gabby, shooting her in the head, causing serious brain injury. He kept firing, over and over, shooting eighteen others who had come to speak to their congresswoman. In the end, Loughner had killed Federal Judge John Roll, Gabby staff member Gabe Zimmerman, Dorothy Morris, Phyllis Schneck, Dorwan Stoddard, and nine-year-old Christina-Taylor Green, who went to the event in hopes of talking to Gabby. Several people in the crowd tackled Loughner as he attempted to reload his handgun with another magazine, and held him for sheriff's deputies. A doctor and a nurse who had been shopping in the store began giving medical aid to the injured. A young man, Daniel Hernandez, an intern in Gabby's office, sat with the severely injured Giffords, holding her and trying to stop the bleeding from her head wound.

In the midst of the violence and chaos, everyday citizens

became heroes. Those who rushed toward the armed Loughner to stop him, the woman who dove to the ground to seize the loaded magazine from his hand, and those who began giving aid to the shooting victims all reacted courageously in the face of danger. Because of them no other lives were lost. Loughner was stopped from shooting others and detained for law enforcement. The incredible sadness his actions brought to the community in those few seconds of the shooting had just begun. It would not end with his sentencing.

Sometime after ten thirty, shortly after the shooting, Assistant Tucson Police Chief John Leavitt called me at my home. He told me what limited information law enforcement had at that time. As with any murder, my office would want a prosecutor at the scene. I called my boss, County Attorney Barbara LaWall, and another colleague from work, Chief Criminal Deputy Kellie Johnson. They both said they would head to the scene with me, which by then was secured by dozens of sheriff's deputies.

Every time I go out to a homicide scene, the sense of loss is palpable. No matter the victim, you always realize that they were someone's son or daughter, parent, or partner. I have been to dozens, if not hundreds, of murder scenes over three decades. I've seen murdered children, teens, and adults. I've been to locations where there was more than one victim who had been killed, and exposed to all manner of violent deaths. But never before had it been personal. I had known Judge Roll for over thirty years. He was a kind and patient jurist and had been a prosecutor in my office before I started in the early 1980s. My wife and I had known Gabe Zimmerman's father, Ross, for many years from his work with my wife at the University of Arizona and later from his work in technology in my own office.

Prior to the 2008 election in which Gabby was running for a second term to Congress, my wife and I had hosted a fund-raising party for her at our home. Her office spokesman, Mark Kimble, was then and remains one of my closest friends. Arriving at the scene was emotional. As is typical when a prosecutor is called to a murder, the bodies of most of the deceased were still present, having been covered with sheets because of the large number of people and cars that were still in the parking lot that served the several stores in the outdoor mall. Mark and his wife, Jennifer Boice, were among the first people I saw when I got to the scene. Mark had been at the scene of the shooting but was not injured. Jennifer had driven to the store after being called by Mark. They were standing just inside the crime scene tape that law enforcement had put up to begin preserving the crime scene and to keep people at a distance. Their faces showed shock and sadness. I walked up and put my arms around them and remember telling them that things would be OK. I was at a loss to say more.

By the time I arrived, the injured had all been transported to area hospitals. The news about Gabby was grim. The bullet to her head had entered and exited her brain. Rumors circulated that she was already dead. In fact, we later learned that as Gabby's husband, Mark Kelly, was rushing to Tucson after hearing the news of the shooting, he heard a news broadcast that his wife had died. It was impossible to fully comprehend the fear, shock, and sadness of the victims and their families.

Typically when I go to a homicide scene, I wait until the detectives and forensic workers have finished gathering evidence, taking pictures, and searching for anything and everything that might be important. Once completed, or nearly so, those leading the investigation then walk me through, describing what they had found. Such a procedure helps me, or any prosecutor, in understanding the crime so that charges can be filed, for one, and later during the trial, the firsthand view is beneficial to prosecuting the case. My colleague Kellie and I had prosecuted many cases together, in fact we were scheduled to start three back-to-back trials three days later on a double murder capital case that happened in the town of Arivaca, south of Tucson. We waited outside the grocery store for the sheriff's department, in whose jurisdiction the shooting had occurred, to process the scene. It was to be a long wait.

Because the victims included a federal judge and a US congresswoman, not only was the sheriff's department at the scene but so was the special agent in charge of the local FBI and three assistant US Attorneys from the local office in Tucson. I knew them all and worked with them when all three were prosecutors in my office some years before. We talked about the case, adding details about what we were learning as the investigation proceeded. We stood together and watched as the sheriff's investigative team put on protective gear of booties and gowns to enable them to process the scene without contaminating any potential evidence. Just as the investigators were about to start, the sheriff's commander stopped everyone. A call had just come from then FBI director Robert Mueller that the agency was taking charge of everything because of the federal connections. He was flying from Washington, and local law enforcement was to back out and leave the crime scene to the FBI forensic team.

———•———

Since that team was not there, we waited. The local forensic team, who I had seen examine hundreds of violent crime scenes, stepped away, and I watched them take off the booties and gowns. I was concerned. Not that I thought the FBI wasn't competent, but the local police and sheriff conducted this type of investigation all the time. Local law enforcement had vast experience in preserving, collecting, and processing evidence in violent crime cases. I thought they were simply better suited to handle the case. It brought up another issue, of course. If the feds were going to be conducting the investigation, what office was going to prosecute, mine or the US Attorney? While my friends and colleagues who were federal prosecutors were very good lawyers and knew how to try a case, my office was much more experienced in death penalty prosecutions. This type of mass killing certainly warranted the filing of such a notice.

The immediate compromise was that the FBI would include local detectives in the investigation and the interviews of witnesses. Both the state and federal officers and prosecutors would have access to all the information. Kellie and I stayed actively involved, as we had discussed that while federal jurisdiction clearly covered Gabby and Judge Roll, it seemed to us that we had exclusive jurisdiction for the charges regarding those victims not connected to the federal government. No one had an interest in any sort of battle over who was going to handle the case, just a concern that we follow the law and make sure there was a successful prosecution. Because the shooting had occurred in our county, we had concurrent jurisdiction with the federal government. What that meant was that legally both the state and the federal government could bring charges against Loughner, one indictment in federal court, one in state court. Kellie and I knew that in Arizona this was a death penalty case.

As in any city that has suffered such a violent act, people in Tucson were consumed with the news, horrified, shocked, and saddened. But the emotions were not limited to our community. Four days after the shooting, President Obama came to a memorial service at the University of Arizona. Some fourteen thousand people packed the arena to show support for the victims. Others stood outside, unable to get in. Those who had rushed in to stop the slaughter and render aid were lauded by the president. Obama brought both cheers and tears when he told the crowd that he had gone by Gabby's hospital room before the service. He announced to everyone that while he was there, Gabby had opened her eyes for the first time since being wounded. There were no dry eyes.

Loughner had been taken by the FBI and remained in federal custody. Kellie and I were starting six months of trial in a multiple murder case and were too busy at that point to have much to do with the decisions being made by the feds. The head of the US Attorney's criminal division was a friend of mine and lived in my neighborhood. When we could we'd talk about the case and what the feds thought they could do. They had decided on a unique approach. While there were specific federal statutes about the crimes against a federal judge or member of Congress, in order to include all nineteen victims, the federal prosecutors decided they could cover them because they were all attending a federally sponsored and sanctioned event, the "Congress on Your Corner." In the meantime we reserved our right to indict Loughner on all charges in state court because the shooting happened in our county. None of the decisions were of urgency, as Loughner had been ruled incompetent to stand trial due to his mental illness. The federal judge assigned to the case had sent him to a federal mental health facility to regain competence.

The US Attorney's Office in Tucson had gotten permission from the Department of Justice to file a death penalty allegation in the case, and they did so. Any federal prosecution across the country had to have permission from Washington before any federal murder case could be considered a capital one. However, the case remained in legal limbo until mid-2012. Loughner was being

treated at the federal medical prison, and my office was holding
off on a decision to bring state charges for murder and aggravated
assault. But all that began to change in the summer of that year.

Loughner had been assigned a defense attorney out of California named Judy Clarke. I had never met her, but the cases
she'd handled were legendary. Over the years Judy had represented
Olympic Park bomber Eric Rudolph, Unabomber Ted Kaczynski,
and much later, Dzhokhar Tsarnaev, the man charged with the
Boston Marathon bombing. There were many other high profile
cases she'd handled. While mainly her focus had to do with the case
filed in federal court, she had to be concerned that if she could get a
plea from the feds that my office could take him and subject him to
the death penalty despite any federal plea or sentence. The federal
government could not bind the state to any agreement about the
case. So Judy contacted us.

Judy first contacted me through a mutual friend, a local defense
attorney named Laura Udall. Clarke wanted to know informally
what we might do. I told her that the decision would ultimately
be up to my boss, Barbara LaWall. That decision would be based
on the law, the type of plea entered federally, and the input of the
victims. I told Judy that we should have a meeting here but that
if Loughner was pleading to the rest of his life in prison and the
victims were satisfied with that resolution, I felt my office would
go along with that.

Judy scheduled the meeting with us and flew out from California with a colleague. She told us that Loughner would likely
accept responsibility for everything once he regained competency
and plead guilty to charges that would lock him up for the rest
of his life. He was twenty-two at the time. She provided us with
information about Loughner's background and his mental illness
and asked that we consider that being the end of the case. Barbara

thanked her for the information and told Judy we would have to consider the matter.

That wasn't my only contact with the case in the summer of 2012. My friend, and Gabby's spokesperson, Mark, had persuaded me to go to the Indianapolis 500 race with him and a group of people. I'm not a race fan, but I agreed to go. I actually drove out alone from Tucson, stopping to visit relatives along the way. Mark wanted to drive back with me, stopping in Houston to visit Gabby, where she was recovering. We stopped in, taking breakfast for all of us one morning, on our drive back to Arizona. Mark had seen Gabby since the shooting, but I had not. For someone who'd been shot through the head, she had made tremendous progress.

I wasn't sure Giffords would remember me since it had been a long time since we'd met and of course she was recovering from a serious head wound. On introducing myself at their house, I said she may not remember me but we had met when we'd had the fund raiser at my house in 2008. "Only once," she chided me, "only once." I found her memory and thought process to be remarkable.

———

We only stayed about an hour with Gabby and her husband Mark, but inevitably our discussion led us to the case. I made clear that I was not the prosecutor and that our office had not yet decided whether to bring state charges. I told them that based on my experience and the knowledge I had about the case, I was fairly certain Loughner would offer to plead guilty and agree to the rest of his natural life in prison. Gabby had trouble still with making complete sentences, but she clearly expressed she wanted that outcome. Mark Kelly was more direct. They didn't want to go to trial if life in prison was the option. They, like many victims, wanted to move on.

While Gabby was unable to fully articulate in words the impact of the case on her, she did with action. She had lost friends, colleagues, and constituents in the shooting. She had a long friendship with Judge Roll and had worked with him on federal court issues. I was concerned that our visit might be too tasking for her and felt we should get back on the road. But she wanted me to see one more thing to demonstrate what she'd been through. Gabby stood up from the kitchen table and walked to the freezer. Opening it she pushed aside several frozen packages. Reaching deep into the freezer, she brought out an object sealed in plastic. She placed the portion of her skull that had been removed in surgery into my hand.

It covered my whole hand. To me her message was clear. So much damage had been done. So much grief. It was time to move on.

At the end of the summer, the federal medical facility declared Loughner was competent, and after supporting testimony was given in court, the judge presiding over the case made the ruling that he was legally able to participate in his case. Soon after, Judy Clarke scheduled a hearing to change his plea to guilty. The federal prosecutors had met with the victims and nearly all were in agreement to accept a plea that would put Loughner in prison until he died. My office had yet to decide on state charges, but Judy had sufficient assurances from our discussions that we'd go along with the federal resolution that she could confidently move forward with a plea. On November 8, 2012, Loughner was sentenced. He will never be released.

That left the question of state charges. Barbara had previously met with the victims and listened to their concerns. A prosecution in state court would take years, would involve the same delays in competency issues that the federal courts had experienced, and would give no resolution to the victims beyond what they already had expressed they wanted. After Loughner was sentenced, Barbara met with victims and family members and announced to them that she would not charge him. The room broke into applause.

Less than two years after the shooting, Loughner was sentenced to die in prison with the multiple life sentences he was given. There is more certainty of him remaining in prison for the rest of his life than any death sentence that could have been imposed. The man who killed six, wounded thirteen, will live out his life behind bars.

In the years since, I've written several guest editorials for the local paper on our gun laws. Usually after another mass shooting. Loughner, despite his mental illness, had no trouble buying a handgun equipped with a magazine that could hold more than two dozen bullets. There are many steps we can take to tighten our laws while protecting the rights of gun owners. Gabby started a foundation, Giffords, to promote sensible guns laws nationwide. Someday, perhaps, Gabby and others like her will help prevent shootings like the one that changed her life.

As to the death penalty for Loughner, most of the victims' survivors got the result they wanted: a chance to move on with their lives and not be burdened with years of litigation, a trial that would cause them to relive the most horrific day of their lives, and then, if the state was successful in its quest for a death sentence, years or decades of further appeals and hearings. Here, because my colleagues in the US Attorney's Office decided to accept Loughner's plea, and because my office agreed not to pursue further prosecution, Loughner is locked away for life, and the survivors don't have to think of him again.

12

CLOSURE

While I've written about my own cases in which the arbitrary application of the death penalty could be argued, that is only one issue of concern. There are an endless number of articles, studies, and books about issues such as costs, exonerations, racial disparities, lengthy delays, and so on. A brief look at some of these issues might lead one to seek out other writings that devote much more discussion to them.

Over the last thirty-five years, I've tried over one hundred murder cases. Of those, about twenty were cases in which the state sought the death penalty. Seven inmates are currently on death row. Two others have been executed. Seven more have had their death sentences reduced to life. The reductions to life came about for a variety of reasons. One was after the US Supreme Court held it unconstitutional for a person under the age of eighteen at the time of the offense to have a death sentence imposed on him. One, Wallace, in chapter two, was simply a change in the position of the Arizona Supreme Court. Others came about because their cases were sent back from appeal for some legal technicality, and we decided not to seek a death sentence again but rather agreed to a life sentence. Some cases resulted in the death penalty being dismissed by the prosecution when a more culpable defendant received a lesser sentence. We just felt it equitable.

None were released due to a claim of innocence, but that possibility should give everyone pause. The exact percentage of wrongful convictions that exist in the criminal justice system overall may be debatable, what is not up for debate is that they do exist. While most observers agree that the number is low, conviction of the innocent is a fact. Ray Krone in my own state spent years in prison for a murder until DNA eventually cleared him. In my office a man named Larry Youngblood spent several years in prison for child molestation until DNA identified another man as the true perpetrator.

Across the country there are numerous reported cases of innocent people being arrested and at times imprisoned for crimes they did not commit. In Texas, Michael Morton was imprisoned for over two decades for the murder of his wife, based at least in part on the withholding of evidence by the prosecutor. Most readers will be familiar with the Duke University Lacrosse team case in which an overzealous prosecutor also withheld evidence that would have cleared those who were investigated. Whether by mistaken eyewitness testimony, an unscrupulous prosecutor, a lab mistake, or simply by accident, innocent people are convicted of crimes.

———•+•———

In a US Supreme Court case named *Kansas v. Marsh*, Justice Antonin Scalia addressed head on the issue of an innocent person being sentenced to death. In a lengthy separate opinion in which he concurred with the finding of the majority, Scalia wrote about claims of innocence in several specific cases across the country. In each he noted that the claim had been proven wrong. Famously, he declared that if an innocent person had been executed in the modern era (essentially going back to the 1950s), given the number of people looking for such a person, it would be "shouted from the rooftops by the abolition lobby." Justice Scalia finished his opinion by stating that even based on claims of innocence, when compared to the overall numbers of convictions, that the state gets it right 99.973 percent of the time. Good numbers if you aren't in the other 0.027 percent.

However, the estimates from other studies suggest a much higher number, perhaps as high as 4.1 percent in one study by a Michigan law professor. While these numbers apply to all types of crime, there is no reason to believe they don't hold true for capital cases. The question one must answer then is, if our system allows for wrongful convictions, are we willing to continue to execute convicted murderers? Based on my own experience with dozens upon dozens of prosecutors over more than three decades, the overwhelming majority take pride in doing justice rather than seeking convictions, but it is not difficult to find a case where a prosecutor obtained a conviction because he withheld vital evidence from the defense. Those few cases can cause a lack of confidence in our justice system. While rare, wrongful convictions clearly occur. Are we willing to take the chance of an innocent person being executed? The alternative of life in prison without parole exists. Shouldn't that be sufficient?

Over the years, I've met with countless surviving family members of victims of murder. Most, before the murder of their loved one, had given little thought to the death penalty. Arizona law requires that the prosecutor meet with victims of crime and get their input about the case. However, victims do not get to decide whether to seek the death penalty. The prosecution alone decides. But the prosecutor listens and explains the system. Some people think that a death sentence will give them closure, that the death of the murderer will somehow help the victims' loved ones heal from their grief.

Once they know more about the death penalty system, many survivors are grateful that their case never proceeded as a capital one. I've had family members tell me that once they've seen how death penalty cases are delayed in getting to trial and how the appeals seemingly go on endlessly, that closure was accomplished by a conviction, a life sentence, and moving on with their lives as best they could. Others whose cases ended with the imposition of a death sentence have told me that had they really understood my words to them about delays and decades of appeals, they would have fought hard to keep their case from ever being considered for a death sentence.

Sandy Owen's sister, Janet, told me that the thirty-six years of litigation after her sister's murderers were sentenced to death turned out to be her worst nightmare. Rather than closure, each appeal and court hearing caused Sandy to die over and over. It is a sentiment I've heard many times. Pizza Hut victim Bob Curry's sister, Kathy Weir, speaks once a year to a class I teach on prosecution at the University of Arizona law school. It is still a very emotional subject for her to discuss. Each year she tells the students how, even years later, she is still troubled by the decision to seek death in the Pizza Hut triple murder. If the only sentence under consideration had been life, she is certain that the initial convictions would have been upheld and the cases would have been long closed. Undoubtedly she is correct.

———————

Typically a murder defendant receiving a life sentence gets one appeal. While other types of appeals can be filed post-conviction for a murderer, few are successful, and the case is usually final after three to five years of legal proceedings. A death sentence, however, has appeals that last, in Arizona, an average of seventeen to twenty years. Even then few of the sentences are carried out. In California there are over 740 inmates on death row. In the last forty years, California has had just thirteen executions. In Arizona, there are nearly 120 death row inmates. Since 1992, there have been thirty-four executions. One of my defendants has been on death row since 1992, another since 1996. Both are still appealing their sentences, as are all death row inmates, with court-appointed attorneys. Scott

Clabourne, as I noted in an earlier chapter, has been on death row thirty-five years. The costs can skyrocket.

One can look on the Internet and find dozens of studies about the additional costs incurred when a murder case becomes a capital case. The numbers are all over the map. Anywhere from a conservative estimate of a million dollars more per case and up. In Arizona a defendant is entitled to two court-appointed attorneys. In addition, case law has required that to have effective assistance of counsel, the retention of experts in mental health, mitigation experts to delve into family backgrounds, prison experts, and other expert witnesses is necessary and almost always at taxpayer expense. One elected prosecutor in northern Arizona announced in 2018 that his office was dropping its effort to seek the death penalty in two unrelated murder cases. Citing the expense, the prosecutor stated that the prosecution of the two accused murderers had already cost his county over $2 million, and neither case had yet gone to trial. One example from my own cases might help illustrate this point.

In 2011 Kellie Johnson and I tried three defendants for the murders of a father and his nine-year-old daughter. The killings were horrible, and we sought the death penalty. The murders happened in May 2009. Shawna Forde, Jason Bush, and Albert Gaxiola invaded the home of Raul Flores, his wife, Gina, and their daughter, Brisenia, early in the morning in the small town of Arivaca, Arizona, forty minutes south of Tucson. They hoped to find money and drugs, but all they found was a family sleeping in their home.

Forde wanted to establish a border militia group to patrol the Southern Arizona border with Mexico looking for those crossing illegally. She had been part of a similar group in the past but found them too tame for her liking. She was more militant in her approach and recruited others with a similar mentality. The plan was to finance her group by robbing those who they believed to be drug dealers or others involved in illegal activity. Such a plan brought them to the Flores home at one o'clock in the morning in late May 2009.

Forde and Bush were dressed in camouflage clothing and pounded on the Flores' front door in the middle of the night. They claimed to be border patrol and were looking for migrants who had crossed the border illegally. Raul at first asked them to wait until he could get dressed, but Bush pointed a gun at him threatening to shoot if Raul moved. Bush and Forde entered the home. Brisenia had fallen asleep in the living room with a new puppy she had just gotten as a present. Upon hearing the commotion, Gina had come into the living room, where Bush had Raul covered with a .45-caliber handgun.

Forde and Bush demanded to know where the money was and where the drugs were. Raul responded that they had neither, and Bush shot him six times with the handgun, killing him. Bush turned his gun on Gina, shooting her in the chest and the leg. Gina fell, her leg broken by the bullet, and she was bleeding from the chest wound. Brisenia woke to the noise and began screaming when she saw her parents shot and not moving. Bush walked over to Brisenia, put his .45-caliber handgun to her head, and shot the nine-year-old twice, immediately killing her. Gina was still alive, conscious, and only a few feet from her husband and daughter.

Gina could hear drawers and cabinets being searched through-out the house. Not finding anything, the invaders left. Gina was able to crawl from the living room to a phone in the kitchen, where she called 9-1-1. Bush and Forde, however, had left an AK-47 in the house, and Forde reentered to retrieve it. Upon entering Forde saw Gina on the phone and ordered Bush and Gaxiola, who Gina had not yet seen, to go back into the house and finish her off. With Gina on the phone in the kitchen, Bush went to one entryway and began firing at Gina with his .45. Gaxiola, at another entryway, began shooting at Gina with a shotgun. Gina was able to reach her husband's handgun stored in a cabinet in the kitchen and return fire. All this was captured on the 9-1-1 tape. While somehow both Bush and Gaxiola missed Gina, she managed to shoot Bush in the leg.

When Gina returned fire, both Bush, now injured and bleeding, and Gaxiola fled. The two left the scene, along with Forde, leaving behind the AK-47 and Bush's blood that drained from his wound as he ran across the yard with the other two. While they escaped that day, the investigators identified them, and all three were under arrest within a matter of days. Because of the nature of the crime, two murdered including the nine-year-old Brisenia, and the attempted murder of Gina, my office sought the death penalty.

For the three defendants, there were six defense attorneys appointed. In addition, for purposes of the sentencing portion of the trial should any of them be convicted, each defendant was able to hire a mitigation specialist—a type of social worker who investigates the defendant's family background, schooling, and basically everything about his or her life. Each defendant hired either a psychologist or psychiatrist to investigate any potential mental health issues and testify to the jury. There is a cottage industry nationwide of experts of all sorts who testify around the country in death penalty cases. The testimony ranges from mental health issues and family histories to how well the defendant can be controlled in prison should the jury give life instead of the death penalty. It's expensive and paid for by the taxpayer.

In 2011, Kellie and I tried the three defendants in back-to-back trials, each with a separate jury. It took nearly six months. In the end the juries for Bush and Forde imposed the death penalty for each of them. The jury for Gaxiola imposed a life sentence.

None of the juries were allowed to know the outcome of the other defendants' cases but arrived at their own decisions. In the end, the defense cost to the county for the three trials was $1 million. That was just the beginning.

———————

For purposes of appeal, defendants are appointed new lawyers. Bush got two. There was no question of his guilt. His DNA was all over the crime scene from the gunshot wound inflicted when Gina returned fire. In addition, when he was found hiding in a small town in northern Arizona, Bush fully confessed to the murders and described how he shot both Raul and Gina. Nonetheless, he is, of course, entitled to an appeal. As of 2017, Bush was on his first appeal, called a direct appeal, to the Arizona Supreme Court. The county agency that funds the lawyers and costs of appealing these cases has spent, at this early stage, an additional $450,000 for lawyers and investigators for Bush. His first appeal had not concluded by the end of 2018. Should the court affirm his conviction and sentence, he is likely to have court-appointed lawyers for the next twenty years.

In late 2017, Bill Montgomery, the elected county attorney in Maricopa County, where Phoenix is located, wrote an opinion piece for the daily newspaper in Phoenix entitled "Why Arizona Still Needs the Death Penalty." Montgomery is a longtime prosecutor, intelligent and ethical. He cited the thorough and deliberative process prosecutors go through to decide whether a murder case should be elevated to a capital one. He wrote about the need for capital punishment for the rare horrific murder reflecting the worst of the worst of murderers and cited the fact that national polls still show continued support for the death penalty. While I agree with him about the deliberative process and the national polls, I think there is much more to be said about the continued need to put killers to death.

Arizona's supreme court has had a commission for some years to study the current state of capital litigation around Arizona. In December 2018, the members submitted their latest report to the court with some sobering statistics. In the ten years preceding the report, there were fifty-nine sentences of death imposed. But that was out of hundreds of cases statewide that started out as capital ones. Just taking the years 2008 to 2014 and ignoring the numbers from 2015 to 2018 to account for the length of time it takes to get such a case to trial, there were over 750 cases in Arizona that started out as death penalty cases. While many may have pled or perhaps had the death notice withdrawn before trial, the numbers show an overwhelming rejection of the sentence by most juries and a phenomenal waste of resources.

As of 2018, there are thirty states that allow for capital punishment. But many of those states have either not executed a murderer in many years, or the punishment has simply fallen into disuse. In fact, a handful of counties around the country have been involved in a large percentage of the capital litigation pending in courthouses at any given time. While polling suggests that a slight majority of the country supports the continued use of the death penalty, those numbers drop when the polling provides for a natural life sentence as an option to death. The problem with any polling, however, is that people are asked about their opinions regarding capital punishment when few have any real-life experience with how it works, who it applies to, what it costs, the lengthy delays, and the impact it has on victims. Whether the poll results would be different with full knowledge of our capital system is an unanswered question.

What I've tried to do by writing about some of my own cases is to give some context to the question of whether we need to continue having the death penalty. There are unquestionably evil people in our world who commit unspeakable and despicable crimes. What we need to answer is whether we should continue to spend resources on a costly process that brings uncertain outcomes to those cases and whether we should have this process for the very few people to which it ultimately applies.

———————

This uncertainty is described by Justice Scalia in the opinion he wrote in *Kansas v. Marsh*. Quoting from a journal article written by a longtime prosecutor and acquaintance of mine, Scalia recognized that because of the heightened scrutiny given to death penalty cases over the years of review by appellate courts, nearly two-thirds of all death sentences are overturned. Not because of innocence but most based on legal errors that some reviewing court has found in its careful scrutiny. In most areas of our lives, if two-thirds of the work we did had to be redone, we'd think carefully about whether we would continue with such an endeavor.

Oftentimes the reversed cases are not again subjected to an attempt on the part of the prosecution to seek a death sentence but rather are pled to a life sentence or a term of years. Those outcomes can leave victims in limbo for years, more culpable defendants with lesser sentences, and decisions reached through the "vagaries of the criminal justice system."

FINAL WORDS

I have attended multiple executions of convicted murderers in Arizona. They are, in a word, bizarre. After years of appeals, in the weeks before a scheduled execution, an inmate can make one last effort to save his life. In Arizona, the Board of Executive Clemency holds a hearing at the prison to listen to anyone who wishes to speak with them about whether the board should recommend to the governor that clemency be granted and the inmate's life spared. Only the governor has the power to actually commute a sentence upon such a recommendation. This hearing comes after appeals in both state and federal courts that spent years analyzing every word spoken at trial, applied case law to every issue raised by the defendant, and rendered a legal opinion that can be dozens of pages long. Yet despite these decades of procedures, the board can recommend that death not be imposed.

The hearings are conducted in a very secure area of the prison, but where access is granted to anyone to simply come watch or, if they choose, to speak to the board. There is no requirement that a person have some connection to the case or the inmate. The inmate is present but in a small cell and guarded by multiple corrections officers. The hearings will typically have presentations by the inmate's lawyers about why the board should recommend clemency, followed by the prosecution's presentation about why the crime shows clemency should not be granted. Victim family members as well as the inmate's family can plead their case to the board. Often there are religious groups in attendance to state their position on the death penalty. Once at a hearing I attended, a man got up to speak, and when asked what he wanted to tell the board, he simply stated that while he knew nothing about the case in question, his family had encouraged him to do some public speaking, so there he was! The board deliberates their decision in the open in front of all in attendance. Typically the decision is against a clemency recommendation.

The day of execution is guided by multiple rules within the prison. By law, the execution must be witnessed by citizens of the state. There are typically four groups in attendance: the victim's family; the defendant's family along with his lawyers and clergy; the media; and the "official" group of prosecutor, law enforcement, and any resident of the state who has requested to be a witness. There are a lot of people, typically in the range of thirty or more, who make up the four groups. These groups are kept in separate areas of the prison and not allowed to see other groups while they wait in their assigned locations. At times my group has had trays of food with sandwiches, cookies, and soft drinks brought in by inmates from the prison kitchen. This always seems odd to me, as I'm not there for lunch and the inmates attempting to serve us know who we are and why we are there. Eating food, especially served by prisoners who know why I'm there, is the last thing I ever plan to do.

After lengthy waits we're taken to a location closer to the execution building, and there we wait again. We still won't be in contact with or even see the other groups. Finally the four groups are led in a single line into the building holding the death chamber. This walk will pass by dormitories housing inmates who can look out and see us being led down the sidewalks. I doubt the prison is ever quieter than on such a day. The silence is truly eerie. Once in the building, those in attendance are directed onto some standing risers, with burly corrections officers doing their best to continue to keep the groups separated despite the small room and one set of risers. Those in attendance typically end up standing next to each other, all semblance of separation being discarded. After a short wait with the exterior door closed, a curtain opens to reveal the inmate already strapped to a gurney, IVs already inserted in his veins, and a sheet pulled up to his neck.

Over the next few minutes, the warden reads the death warrant authorizing the prison to carry out the execution, and he lets those in attendance know that there have been no last-minute reprieves of execution from any court. The inmate is given a chance to make a statement if he wishes. Don Miller, in 2000, looked through the window separating the witnesses from his gurney and told Jennifer's brother that he was sorry for taking his sister from him. Another inmate looked to his attorneys and motioned with two fingers. The media later erroneously reported he had given the "V for victory" sign. In reality he was, as his last act, letting his attorneys know there were two IVs being used by the prison staff, a concern for them about the use of lethal injection and how, at times, the executions have gone horribly wrong. Other inmates I've seen have said very little. The drugs used in the execution are then administered by a person out of eyesight to the witnesses. Typically within minutes the inmate is pronounced dead. Oddly, state law requires an autopsy to determine the cause of death despite the many witnesses to the act.

Executions are rare enough, at least in Arizona, such that the media reports on them extensively. At Don Miller's execution, it even brought in some national news figures. I was standing next to a local television reporter and next to her was a man from a national news show. As Miller was pronounced deceased, this national reporter turned to our local reporter and me and announced he had just seen Miller's soul leave his body. Neither of us replied.

That's it. After lengthy trials, years of appeals, countless sums being spent, and media coverage of the execution, it ends with the inmate dying. The witnesses shuffle out, return to their cars, and drive away. The ending is anticlimactic. The execution has not brought back the victim of course and, with few exceptions, has not brought anyone any satisfaction. Families continue to try to survive their loss, but I'm yet to be told that an execution has brought closure.

The death penalty is given to very few murderers. The sentence is carried out on even fewer. Between sentence and execution, the state spends millions of dollars on each case where the death penalty was given, yet it is more likely that a particular murderer will escape his sentence through a retrial or some other legal technicality. Even Justice Scalia, a death penalty supporter, recognized that fact. He described our capital jurisprudence (case law decided by the courts) as "incoherent." Justice Samuel Alito has more charitably called it "exceedingly complex."

Justice Harry Blackmun wrote that he was optimistic that the Supreme Court eventually would conclude that the effort to eliminate arbitrariness in capital cases, while preserving fairness, is so plainly doomed that the death penalty would be abandoned. He wrote that in 1994. Who dies and who lives is a decision that becomes the arbitrary application of convoluted statutes and conflicting and inconsistent court decisions, as one of my judges announced. I think he was right.

APPENDIX

Some may wish to read the appellate cases about the defendants in the chapters of the book. Most are available on the Internet and sites like Westlaw and LexisNexis, where the published opinions can be found. Some of the cases are only what are termed memorandum decisions that did not make it into the state or federal reporters. Where there is an opinion, I cite that below. Memorandum decisions are cited with the court citation.

Chapter One: Sandy
Smith v. Ryan, 813 F.3d 1175 (9th Cir. 2016)
State v. Smith, 138 Ariz. 79 (1983)
State v. Lambright, 138 Ariz. 63 (1983)
Lambright v. Schriro, 490 F. 3d 1103 (9th Cir. 2007)

Chapter Two: Susan, Anna, and Gabriel
State v. Wallace, 151 Ariz. 362 (1986)
State v. Wallace, 229 Ariz. 155 (2012)
Wallace v. Stewart, 184 F. 3d 1112 (1999)

Chapter Three: Jennifer
State v. Miller, 186 Ariz. 314 (1996)

Chapter Four: Virginia
State v. Bertsch, No. 2 CA-CR-95-0349
(Ariz. Ct. App. April 17, 1997)

Chapter Five: Prosecutor's Decision
Ring v. Arizona, 536 US 584 (2002)

Chapter Six: Gary
State v. Phillips, No. 1 CA-CR-17-0285
(Ariz. Ct. App. May 15, 2018)

Chapter Eight: Melissa, James, Bob
State v. Prasertphong, 206 Ariz. 70 (2003)
State v. Huerstel, 206 Ariz. 93 (2003)

Chapter Nine: Laura
State v. Clabourne, 142 Ariz. 335 (1984)

Chapter Ten: Rhia
State v. Alegria, No. 2 CA-CR-2013-0567
(Ariz. Ct. App. March 9, 2016)

Chapter Twelve: Closure
State v. Forde, 233 Ariz. 543 (2014)
Kansas v. Marsh, 548 US 163 (2006)

ABOUT THE AUTHOR

Rick Unklesbay has been a prosecutor with the Pima County Attorney's Office, in Tucson, Arizona, since 1981 In that time he has tried more than two hundred cases, including over one hundred first degree murder trials. Twenty of the murder trials were death penalty cases. He has received numerous awards, including Arizona Prosecutor of the Year, a trial advocacy award from the Association of Government Attorneys in Capital Litigation and was named Outstanding Trial Prosecutor by the National District Attorney's Association. In 2009 he was one of the first prosecutors ever to be inducted into the American College of Trial Lawyers. Mr. Unklesbay lectures on the death penalty to community groups and school classes and teaches a class on prosecution and criminal law at the University of Arizona James E. Rogers College of Law.